Traditional Tarot

In Focus

Tarot re-imagined for Modern Times!

Traditional Tarot

In Focus

Tarot re-imagined for Modern Times!

Joylina Goodings

Zambezi Publishing Limited
www.zampub.com

First published in 2022 in the UK by Zambezi Publishing Ltd
Plymouth, Devon PL2 2EQ
Tel: +44 (0)1752 367 300   Fax: +44 (0)1752 350 453
email: info@zampub.com   www.zampub.com

Text copyright ©2022 Joylina Goodings
Joylina Goodings has asserted the moral right to be identified as the author of this work.

British Library Cataloguing in Publication Data:
A catalogue record for this book is available from the British Library

ISBN(13) 978-1-903065-90-7
"The Traditional Tarot Deck" card images:
Courtesy of Joylina Goodings, copyright © 2022
Cover image copyright © 2022 Jan Budkowski,

Typesetting by Zambezi Publishing Ltd, Plymouth UK

All rights reserved. No part of this publication may be reproduced, stored in a retrieval system, or transmitted in any form or by any means, electronic, mechanical, photocopying, recording or otherwise, whether currently existing or yet to be developed, without the prior written permission of the publisher. This book is sold subject to the condition that it shall not, by way of trade or otherwise, be lent, resold, hired out or otherwise circulated without the publisher's prior written consent, in any form of binding, cover or format other than that in which it is originally published, and without a similar condition being imposed on the subsequent purchaser.

Disclaimer:- This book is intended to provide general information regarding the subject matter, and to entertain. The contents are not exhaustive and no warranty is given as to accuracy of content. The book is sold on the understanding that neither the publisher nor the author are thereby engaged in rendering professional services, in respect of the subject matter or any other field. If expert guidance is required, the services of a qualified professional should be sought.

Readers are urged to access a range of other material on the book's subject matter, and to tailor the information to their individual needs. Neither the author nor the publisher shall have any responsibility to any person or entity regarding any loss or damage caused or alleged to be caused, directly or indirectly, by the use or misuse of information contained in this book. If you do not wish to be bound by the above, you may return this book in original condition to the publisher, with its receipt, for a refund of the purchase price.

About the Author

Joylina is an inspirational speaker, life coach, counselor, angel expert, psychic clairvoyant, healer, teacher and author.

She became a Reiki Master Teacher in 1997 and gave up her career in professional services marketing in 2000, to use her life-coaching and counseling skills to help people with their personal and spiritual development. Joylina does this by giving readings, life/soul coaching, teaching and healing. She taught at the College of Psychic Studies in London as well as travelling to many spiritual energy spots around the world, leading spiritual holiday workshops and retreats.

Joylina has served as President of the British Astrological and Psychic Society (BAPS), and has been responsible for creating and updating many of their courses, as well as assessing prospective new members. She is now a consultant member of MBS Professionals Ltd, a new body that has taken over BAPS' functions after it sadly closed its doors recently. Joylina believes avidly in maintaining high ethical standards and integrity within her chosen fields of personal and spiritual development.

The author of four books - including the acclaimed "Your Angel Journey" and "In Focus: Auras" - Joylina has another book in progress. She now focuses her energy on writing and developing her online training courses.

While caring for her parents and grandchildren, Joylina enjoys walking along the beautiful Jurassic Coast in Dorset, where she has currently made her home.

Contents

Introduction..3

Chapter One: Tarot Through the Ages 4

Chapter Two: Spiritual Development and Intuition 9

Chapter Three: Choosing & Caring for your Cards..............14

Chapter Four: Colour..19

Chapter Five: Numerology and the Tarot..........................24

Chapter Six: Symbolism 29

Chapter Seven: Introduction to the Major Arcana..............32

Chapter Eight: The Major Arcana....................................34

Chapter Nine: The Minor Arcana.....................................78

Chapter Ten: The Court Cards 123

Chapter Eleven: Giving a Reading 155

Chapter Twelve: Spreads 159

Conclusion..169

Index 170

Introduction

The interpretations in this book are linked to normal life and to the problems we experience every day. This makes the book a great starting point if you are new to the cards, but it also works for those who have only encountered modern spins on the Tarot, and who now fancy discovering deeper meanings. This book will also help you if you are keen to develop your intuition.

With the ever-increasing uncertainties of life and the growing desire to take back some form of control or direction, it is no surprise that there are probably as many books about the Tarot as there are actual Tarot decks. With all this information, it can be easy to feel overwhelmed - not only when learning about the cards, but also when trying to understand the esoteric meanings embedded within them. This book sets out to resolve that problem.

To fully benefit from the Tarot, you need to focus on two things; learning the basic meaning that each card conveys and exercising your intuition. This book will take you through the cards, giving you their core meanings and how they relate in a reading. Equally important, I will give you a handful of simple tools that will help you to develop your intuitive powers. Together, they will be the basis of great readings and a deeper understanding of what life and the Tarot can teach you.

This book is for anyone with a genuine interest in living life to the full. Read what I share with you in this book and practise it until it becomes second nature, and soon you will be uncovering the answers that you seek to truly make a difference in your life.

Chapter One: Tarot Through the Ages

When you pick up a pack of playing cards to play poker, bridge, canasta, rummy or any other card game, little do you realise that you are picking up a modern version of the part of a Tarot deck known as the Minor Arcana. This is why some people can "read" a modern pack of playing cards.

There are two parts to a Tarot deck: The Major Arcana and the Minor Arcana. The Major consists of 22 cards, and the Minor 56 cards, grouped into four suits. The table below shows the similarity between Tarot and playing cards.

Tarot Cards	Playing Cards
Swords	Spades
Cups (or Chalices)	Hearts
Wands (or Rods, Sticks or Staves)	Clubs
Pentacles (or Coins)	Diamonds

When people think of Tarot cards, they usually think of the occult, mysticism and divination. This isn't surprising, because the true origins of the cards are still cloaked in mystery. This has resulted in nearly as many theories about the cards' origins as there are different types of decks and different interpretations of the cards.

The symbolism of the cards and the esoteric and metaphysical doctrines they represent cross the boundaries of different schools of knowledge and teachings. Many believe the cards have their roots in the mystery schools of ancient Egypt, classical Greece, ancient Rome, China or India. Others say they were invented in the 14th century by an Italian noble as a deck of cards in their own

1: Tarot through the Ages

right. Over the centuries, many people believed that the cards were evil, mainly through a lack of understanding of how they worked. Some say, "magic is just undiscovered science" and in this case, it's true.

Some people believed (and still seem to think) that knowledge is power, so they did their best to make the Tarot secret and limit the knowledge to a chosen few, while also exaggerating it into something that it is not. Tarot became feared because the vast majority didn't understand it.

In my youth, I was terrified of all things esoteric and of Tarot in particular. Still, as I grew older, I thought it must be illogical to expect the cards to work, because if you shuffle the cards and lay them out, they will say one thing. If you do it again, the cards will say something else.

When I was invited to learn the Tarot, I set out to prove it didn't work, but now, not only do I read Tarot professionally, but I teach and write about it. So, this is a testament to the way that knowledge enables us to let go of fear.

Possible Links To Tarot Origins
In the absence of much categoric evidence, a game as popular as the Tarot has given rise to numerous claims and ideas regarding its origin, name or the symbols. Over the years, influential people have even changed the meanings and order of some of the cards. A genuinely in-depth discussion is beyond the scope of this book, but an Internet search will furnish as much detail as you may wish to absorb.

Historical Facts
Despite all the speculation about Tarot's origins, there are some

Traditional Tarot In Focus

historical facts worth considering. Evidence exists to show that the Tarot came to Europe in the early to mid-1300s. In 1332, history records that Alphonse XI, King of Leon and Castile, banned all cards – although there is no specific reference to the Tarot. Records show that in the mid-1300s, a monk called Johannes of Brefeld described a popular card game that included images of kings and knights. In 1377, Johannes Von Rheinfelden of Switzerland wrote an essay in which he referred to a game of cards: "...in which game, the state of the world as it is now is most excellently described and figured. But at what time it was invented, where, and by whom, I am entirely ignorant." He describes something like the playing cards we know today, with fifty-two cards in four suits. In 1392, the household accounts of Charles VI of France record a payment being made to Jacquemin Gringonneur, "For three packs of cards, to be gilded and coloured and ornamented with various devices and supplied to the King for his amusement". Seventeen of these cards are today preserved in the Bibliotheque Nationale in Paris.

Records dating back to 1425 appear to show that the Tarot was invented by wealthy Italian classes as a game. The basic rules of the "Tarot" game appear in an Italian manuscript of Martiano da Tortona. We know that cards like the Tarot were used in Italy in the fifteenth century in a popular game called Tarocchi (known as Trumps). The game is a sort of distant cousin to bridge, and it was popular for a time among the royalty in Italy. The pack consisted of more than one hundred cards, and it included signs of the zodiac and the so-called Christian Virtues.

Consequently, designs can be seen to have incorporated the social and religious themes of the day. Early versions of these cards were all individually hand-made. In 1423, St Bernadino of Siena, a celebrated Franciscan preacher, denounced all cards as the creation of Satan, and puritanically minded people all over Europe followed his lead.

Although little reference can be found regarding Tarot cards during the sixteenth and seventeenth centuries, it seems a great many cards were being invented for educational purposes. In 1509,

1: Tarot through the Ages

Thomas Murner designed a pack of sixteen suits intended to teach logic, and later, another deck was created for the teaching of law. In 1603, a German deck was produced that depicted scenes from the Bible, and a deck produced in Paris in 1644 carried scenes from Greek mythology, complete with explanatory notes.

A pack printed in England in 1692 was used to teach the art of carving meat and fish. The King of Hearts is shown dealing neatly with a sirloin of beef, and the King of Clubs dissects a pickled herring!

In 1704, a priest named Menestrier suggested that Gringonneur was the original inventor of Tarot cards and that he devised them to divert Charles VI of France during the unfortunate king's recurrent fits of madness.

The first record of Tarot being associated with the occult is attributed to Antoine Court de Gebelin, a relatively obscure protestant pastor and Parisian mason who wrote about the deck in 1781, three years before his own death. He is said to have "discovered" many of the common myths about the Tarot, such as its origins in ancient Egypt, with the Major Arcana being related to the Qabala.

Even now, cards are used as a fun and straightforward way to teach all sorts of subjects. I remember using "flashcards" to teach my children to read.

Eliphas Levi, in the 1850s, first gave the Tarot its essential place in occultism. He also thought the Martinists and Rosicrucians of the late eighteenth century had best understood the true meaning of the Tarot. Some English mystics now became involved, like Samuel Liddell Mathers, whose mistranslation of Levi brought us the suit of pentacles, while others were Arthur Edward Waite and Aleister Crowley. These people created a large body of writing on the use of the Tarot. For the most part, they thought divination was a "lower" use of the cards, and that ideally, they should be used to understand the eternal mysteries of life. However, divination has always been the most popular use for the cards.

In 1910, Arthur Edward Waite and Pamela Colman Smith introduced what is now the most popular Tarot deck in the world - *The Rider-Waite Tarot*, and the mystic world of the Tarot became available to everyone.

* * *

Tarot images contain universal and archetypal symbols from around the world that embody the great human spiritual journey. A picture speaks a thousand words, and the symbolism easily translates across language and cultural barriers. The symbols are recognisable to Eastern and Western mystics alike, and they connect many mystical and esoteric traditions across the globe. The Tarot, with its rich layers of symbolism, imagery and ancient wisdom, still contains ideas that time and various cultures have failed to suppress.

Whatever the origin, Tarot operates from a world of symbolic imagery that enables us to access conscious and unconscious knowledge. Tarot is a helpful tool for understanding ourselves, others and our world. Today, there are thousands of different Tarot decks available. The symbolism and names of some cards sometimes differ, but the awe and wonder remain. The Catholic Church banned the Tarot and denounced it as evil in the middle ages, and it is still denounced today.

Chapter Two:
Spiritual Development and Intuition

THE FOOL'S JOURNEY

Spiritual self-development is the specific role of the twenty-two cards of the Major Arcana. The Fool follows the journey of life through the archetypal energies and rites of passage demonstrated by the other twenty-one cards until they reach the completion of a cycle. Then the cycle starts from the beginning again, but with increased knowledge and wisdom. The Fool represents the essence of *potential;* so, they follow their inner calling and go forth into the unknown to explore and experience life, see what they are made of, stretch themselves, and achieve their full potential. There are twenty-one rites of passage - each of which is necessary for the soul's evolution.

We see the first half of the journey as "active", where the Fool travels along, seeking knowledge. People struggle to gain their own place in the world, and experience conflicts between their emerging will, ego, mind and emotions. They embark on the journey to discover their individual identity – who they are and who can they become. It is where they evaluate what they have taken on board from their culture, society and parental background, and where they begin to explore their own individual ideals. This often leads to conflict within themselves and with others, as they must reconcile their inner ideals with the reality of the daily world. It connects with the idea that the younger generation often rebels against what has gone before.

This is followed by their passage through maturity, as they balance their experience of living with the reality of the outside world. They are balancing their ego with their knowledge, emotions and dreams as they progress through maturity towards old age. As they continue the journey towards old age, they begin to contemplate the greater meaning of life, and how this affects the different realities they have experienced so far. It is a re-evaluation of life and its lessons, and a search for an inner truth. This is followed by a journey through the darkness that will strip away illusions, both within the world and within the self. This could be called the mid-life crisis. Now they renew their energy and reignite hope, faith, trust and intuition. Slowly things become more transparent as they weigh up everything that has happened in their lives. They proceed towards the light of understanding and the certainty that the cycle is about to begin again. This is the journey of the Major Arcana, the journey of the self to the soul, and it is sometimes called the *Journey to Enlightenment*.

The Minor Arcana also has a role to play, because each card holds symbolism and meaning to help us understand the bigger picture, but this will be covered in more detail later.

Intuition and the Tarot

The most accepted use of the Tarot is divination, where someone asks a question and the cards give them an answer. An intuitive reader will use senses, gut feelings and the literal meaning of a card to feel the way to what a particular card means for a specific person. Like everything else in life, the more we use the muscle of our intuition, the stronger it becomes.

It's the reader's intuitive gift and his interpretation of the cards that make a reading work. The more you read and the more you learn, especially about symbolism, the more you realise there are no fixed rules. There are many different ideas out there, and eventually, everyone develops their own unique style of reading, based on their own thoughts, intuitive feelings and life experiences.

Developing your Intuition or Sixth Sense

Intuition is our innate ability to sense the world around us. It is intuitive or unconscious knowledge that has nothing to do with reason and logic's cognitive skills. It lets us know when there is danger around us, and it can alert us to the true nature of people we meet. It is an innate ability that defies logic. For example, the concept of first impressions, when we take to someone right away, or we take an instant dislike to them, or we are wary of them. This is our intuition at work. It's that uncomfortable feeling that

2: Spiritual Development & Intuition

something is wrong, even though we can't put our finger on it.

Don't confuse being intuitive with being psychic or mediumistic. You don't have to be a medium or a psychic to read the Tarot, but the more you meditate on the cards and develop your intuition, it's likely that you'll develop these abilities as well.

It is often the case that a phone rings and you just know who will be on the other end before you answer it, or letters cross in the post. Psychic ability is just a deeper level of intuitive knowledge. Intuitives and psychics are extremely sensitive to what is known as "the field", which we call the energies around people, found in their auras. There is an energy field surrounding all living organisms, but it is also part of the unconscious mind and even the collective unconscious. An intuitive person just "knows" without knowing how they know.

When developing our intuition, we are, in fact, developing all our senses: sight, smell, hearing, sensing and tasting. We use all our senses unconsciously every day, and becoming intuitive just means that we take more notice of things and act on the information we receive through each of our senses. When we combine all our senses, they form our inner knowing, commonly referred to as our "sixth sense".

Our senses stretch out far beyond our thoughts and out into the surrounding area, which in turn becomes conscious in our mind. Smell is a powerful sense, and it will often take us back to the past. For example, cloves can remind us of visits to the dentist, wintergreen sweets or mulled wine enjoyed while sitting in front of a fire. We are all different, but each memory brings with it an image, a smell, or a sound that conveys feelings. Visual images are often a big part of the way we communicate with ourselves and each other. For this reason, the more widely we read and the more we learn about such things as colour and meditation, the wider the repertoire of images and memories we can tap into and intuit to find deeper meanings in the cards. Like all muscles in the body, we need to use our intuition, or it can dry up and blow away.

Have You Ever...?

- Taken an instant dislike to someone even though they appear nice and friendly?
- Known who was at the end of the line when the phone rings?
- Dreamed of someone you haven't thought of for years and then bumped into them?
- Seemed to "know" how someone is feeling?
- Had "gut feelings" about something that turns out to be correct?

* * *

A Helpful Breathing Meditation

The best way to start your development is with a breathing meditation. Give yourself some quiet time, and focus on your breathing... in and out, in and out... notice how it feels in your nostrils. Is the air warm or cold? How does it feel as your chest rises? Are you breathing from your stomach? How does it feel as you breathe out? As you breathe, start to notice what you can smell in the air around you. Are there flowers, gasoline fumes or pine trees? Notice what you can smell in the air you are breathing, and then focus on what you can hear. Is there traffic? Are there birds singing? And as you focus on your hearing, expand your consciousness into the distance. What can you hear in the distance? What do you notice in the distance?

    You can do this exercise anywhere and at any time because it is just about focusing on what you can sense around you. As you practise, you will become increasingly aware of the sensations within your body, and you will begin to sense more and more.

    We have all heard of or experienced things such as deciding to travel a different way to work and later discovering that we would have been in a bad accident if we had taken our usual route. We may veer to one side for no apparent reason, only to notice soon afterwards that a car was about to run us down. Many people are just "too busy" to notice, but the more we develop our sixth sense and learn to trust our intuition, the more alert we will be.

2: Spiritual Development & Intuition

Expanding your senses and noticing how you feel will help you make decisions because you can ask yourself how something feels, rather than relying on pure logic. For example, asking yourself, "Should I stay in my current job or take the new one that I have just been offered?" Noticing how you feel will tell you what is "right" for you.

When looking into a new job situation, your senses should be filled with energy, and you should feel excited and a bit fearful, but if you feel flat or even somewhat uneasy, the job offer is probably wrong for you. The cells in your body "know" intuitively what you need.

A somewhat weird but prevalent example is suddenly fancying something specific to eat. We don't know why we want it, but our bodies urge us to take in a particular nutrient contained in that food.

* * *

You can do many other exercises to develop each of your senses, but all you need is to focus your attention on each sense individually and take notice. Really notice what something looks like, smells like, sounds like or tastes like and how this "feels" in your body. Notice flowers, birds, trees, people, and especially how food and drink smell and taste. As you practise within your everyday life and expand your senses, you will automatically become much more intuitive than an average Tarot reader who only goes by the meanings of the cards, but a *great* Tarot reader who gains as much or more information from intuition as from the cards. For instance, if you see a spread that is full of Cup cards (more about the suits later), you can immediately see that there is a great deal of emotion surrounding the client's situation. Suppose, for example, you consider the Justice card. In that instance, not everyone who draws it will be involved in a court case, so this is where the extra level of intuition allows you to interpret the specific person's indications for whom you are reading.

Chapter Three:
Choosing & Caring for your Cards

There are many different Tarot decks to choose from, so how do you select the cards that are right for you? This is a question that keeps coming up among those who want to learn the Tarot, but in the end, each one of us is unique, and we all develop our own unique way of reading the cards. We all have our own energy, and each deck of cards has its own energy. It is essential that you feel "drawn" to the imagery of the cards you intend to use. The imagery must speak to you, and it must elicit an emotional response as well as an intellectual one, so you must be drawn to the artwork on the cards.

Some decks are simplistic, colourful and easy to read, such as the Rider Waite deck, along with the large assortment of decks based on this deck, such as the Diamond Tarot. Others are more complex and darker, like the Thoth deck by Aleister Crowley. Some decks focus on individual areas of interest, such as the Egyptian Tarot, the Crystal Tarot, the Oceanic Tarot, the Fountain Tarot, Hermetic Tarot and the Syrian Star Seed Tarot. I think the Osho Zen Tarot is particularly good if you want to use Tarot for self-development and spiritual development.

As you become more familiar with reading the cards, you may well find you are drawn to several different decks, and you may use other decks for various purposes. However, you need to choose a deck to work with for the time being, and I suggest something simple.

PREPARING YOUR CARDS

Once you have bought your cards, it is time to become familiar with them and prepare them. They are going to be important to you, and you need to treat them with respect. Some people like rituals and some don't. There are no hard and fast rules, and it is a personal choice, but ritual can help you focus your mind and

3: Choosing & Caring for your Cards

intention, thus helping to create a sacred environment in which to work. Rituals don't need to be flashy or cumbersome; they just need to mean something to you. Whether it is focusing on your breathing and ensuring you are calm, lighting a candle, burning incense, or making a short prayer to the deity of your choice – it's all fine. In my experience and that of many others, a short personal ritual helps focus your mind and *intention,* and it creates a relaxed environment within which you can proceed.

You need to make a new deck your own by holding the cards in your hands and imagining your energy flowing through the deck. Some people create rituals that they follow every time they pick up the cards; for example, holding the intention of opening the cards and then counting them to make sure they are all there. Most just say an internal prayer, such as asking them to guide you for your highest good. Others may place a crystal on the top of the deck, holding the deck's intention to be cleansed and energised, ready for use. This can be particularly useful when you are doing many readings in a day with many different clients. The crystal can then remove the energy of the last client and prepare the deck for the next one.

When the cards have been energised, you need to decide how and where you intend to store them. Many readers wrap their cards in a silk scarf or keep them in a drawstring bag. The colour of the scarf or bag is up to you, but colours have different meanings which we will cover in a future chapter. Some place them in a special wooden box; others keep them in the box they bought them in. How you choose to keep your cards is entirely up to you. Many people also like to use a special cloth to cover their table or work area, but this is also your own choice.

First Acquaintance

Now it is time to start becoming familiar with the cards. Leave this book to one side and start to develop your personal interpretation; a book like this is precious, but the way the cards speak to you is also vital.

Traditional Tarot In Focus

At this point, you might want to start making notes to refer back to later, and do be sure to congratulate yourself on your progress as you look back on your notes, because you need to see your growth and achievements at any point. Even after all these years of doing professional readings, I still find new interpretations of the cards, so for me and you, making notes helps the absorption of information.

- Pick up a card and look at it.
- What do you notice about it first, what next, then what else?
- What is the general feel of the card?
- How does the card make you feel; happy, sad or fearful?
- What do your senses and your intuition tell you about the card?
- Are there any symbols on the card? If so, what are they, and what do they mean to you?

The same card can come up on more than one day, but you could be drawn to a different part of the card than you were on a previous occasion. Whatever you notice will be the card's significance for you on that day. When you first start to read Tarot, you may be confused, but when this happens, focus all your attention and energy on the card and ask your intuition to tell you what the card is saying for you or the person you are reading for today. As your knowledge of symbols, numbers and colour expands, you will learn to read more into each card.

Changing Views
As time goes on, we tend to change our views and interpretations of each card. We learn new meanings, hear other points of view and we experience the card ourselves. An exciting way to see this is to choose a card and think about how it applied to you at various points in your life, such as in childhood, adolescence, young adulthood and the present. As you progress

3: Choosing & Caring for your Cards

through this book and move into your future, you will continue to find other meanings in each card. Many people find meditating on each card helps them to connect to the card in more profound ways. Some sleep with a card under their pillow at night and seem to intuitively know more about it when they wake. How you get to know your cards is up to you, but I recommend that you don't rush the process.

The Daily Reading

Shuffle the deck and draw a single card in the morning. Ask the card to show you what it means for you today. Notice how the card makes you feel, giving special notice to any part of the card that catches your eye. Make a few notes and at the end of the day, review your notes and see how accurate you were.

Once you begin doing daily readings, you will find specific groups of cards coming up repeatedly, and these could be telling you about your particular concerns. They may also indicate that you need to search more deeply into their meaning.

How you shuffle and cut the deck for your daily card is entirely up to you. Many people shuffle with a question in mind; others just shuffle and ask for an overview. Some cut the cards into two or three piles and then take either the bottom or the top card from any pile. There is no right or wrong way, just what feels comfortable for you. The most crucial step in learning to read any cards, especially Tarot, is to regularly take the cards out of the box. Daily reading is the ideal solution. If you do one reading every day, you will absorb the essence of each card's energy quickly and easily.

THE MINOR ARCANA

The other fifty-six cards are known as the Minor Arcana, and these are broken into four suits representing the following aspects of life:

Swords

These represent our thoughts, creativity, ideas and imagination, and the element of air.

Cups
(Sometimes known as Chalices)
These represent our emotions, our feelings and the element of water.

Wands
(Sometimes referred to as Rods or Staves)
These are the actions we take and represent the element of fire.

Pentacles
(Sometimes referred to as Coins)
These represent our achievements, what we manifest in our lives by combining the other three, and they are the element of earth.

This is the process we go through when manifesting anything in our lives: We have an idea, and if it feels good, we act, thus bringing it into the physical realm. This applies to anything and everything, whether designing a new home, getting a new job, or drawing a quality into your life, such as love or compassion.

General Knowledge

Expand your own personal knowledge and experience because this will influence your understanding of the cards, improving the quality of your readings. The interpretation that you put on a card depends upon what you intuitively feel about it at that moment. You may be drawn to a colour or a symbol within a card, but you need to understand the symbolism of colour in your own culture and in that of others to make sense of it. The broader your general knowledge, the more depth you will be able to bring to your readings.

Chapter Four:
Colour

At this stage, we need to breakdown the different elements of the cards and bring some of your unconscious feelings and instincts into conscious knowledge. The artwork on each card is made up of colour, symbols and numbers as well as the picture itself, all of which invoke feelings within us. Those feeling will be different for each person because we are all unique and we all come from different backgrounds and cultures, all of which form part of our psyche.

COLOURS

It is very difficult to describe a colour, which is why we often use references to the physical and natural world to communicate what a colour looks like, because they act as a point of common experience. Some common examples are grass green, lime green, blood red, sky blue, sunflower yellow and so on. In addition to the shared meanings of colours, you will have personal associations with each shade of colour depending upon your life experiences. Different colours unconsciously affect us each in different ways and invoke different feelings within us. Understanding this is important when reading the cards.

Some colours are known to induce specific types of energy, which is why many large companies decorate their offices with orange colours with a view to energising their staff, without creating the conflict that red can bring. Green is often seen as grounding and warm, whereas blue can be felt as cold, although differing shades induce different feelings.

CHAKRAS AND COLOUR

The chakras belong to a spiritual tradition that originated in India. There are many of them, but the seven main ones line up along the spinal cord and the head, connecting with various glands in the body. The seven chakras have many concepts corresponding to them, including such things as spirituality, mental and emotional needs, and even physical requirements. Each chakra is also associated with a colour that may connect in your mind with the colours that you see on your Tarot deck. There is plenty of information about the chakras on the internet and many books about them, but for the moment, this is a very brief introduction to the chakra system.

Chakra	Colour	Nature
Base or Root	Red	Basic survival requirements.
Sacral	Orange	Relationships, sex, food, satisfaction.
Solar Plexus	Yellow	Will power, physical and mental strength
Heart	Green	Unconditional love.
Throat	Blue	Communication, clairaudience.
Brow or 3rd Eye	Indigo	Clairvoyance and intuition.
Crown	Violet	Link to spirit and higher consciousness.

It is common in Europe and America to wear black as a colour of mourning, but in India, white is the colour of mourning. In Europe, it is common for brides to wear white, but in India, they wear red. It is always important to know what a colour means to you as well as what it may mean to a client.

Colours themselves are neither "good" nor "bad". They are expressions of energy – nothing more. It could be said that "bright" colours mixed with black are "negative", which may be construed as being "bad". This is not necessarily true. It is often necessary and appropriate to suppress or withhold energy to make it more focused within the earth plane. For example, if someone has trouble with expressing their sexuality, dark reds are very good at helping them. Conversely, colours mixed with white are not necessarily more spiritual just because they are more ethereal; a very pale colour can mean wishy-washy. Learning about the way in which you have internalised the meanings of colours yourself is the first step being able to interpret them.

4: Colour

Colour plays a part in all our daily lives, and it can greatly affect our mood – hence the idea of grey days or sunny days. Some colours convey a feeling of calm and others of energy. Seeing the overall colours in the cards and the shades to which you are drawn will give added depth and meaning to your readings.

The lighter the colour, the higher the vibration, so it makes a stronger spiritual connection.

Colour Meanings

Whatever deck you have, the chances are that it will be colourful, so if a particular colour catches your eye, this brief explanation will show you what it's telling you.

Red
You can expect to experience passion for life and there could also be passionate love and passionate lovemaking for you in the near future.

Pink
You will soon receive affection and genuine love from someone whose intentions are good. A connection with a baby girl or female child may be on the way.

Magenta
People will take you seriously at your place of work and you can expect to move up in the organisation.

Pale Blue
If you or your loved ones need healing for the mind and body, it will soon come along. A connection with a baby boy or male child may be on the way.

Traditional Tarot In Focus

Dark Blue
There are serious matters that need your attention, but you must trust your intuition when dealing with them.

Muddy Blue
You will struggle to get your point of view across to others.

Turquoise
You will soon feel mentally and physically healthier and more able to cope with life.

Pale Green
Generosity and love will be around you.

Dark Green
A trip to the countryside will be beneficial.

Muddy Green
Take care, because there is a jealous person around you, and take care that you are not blamed for something you didn't do.

Lavender
You are developing your spirituality and your intuition.

Purple
A strong spiritual connection is on the way, so you may soon receive messages from a spirit guide or feel angels around you.

Pale Yellow
You need more information about something, and you may even need to get some special form of training or education to help you in your job or in your life.

4: Colour

Bright Yellow
You will be determined to finish what you start, and you will also make achievements and become a success.

Orange
You will have the courage needed to deal with anything that comes your way, and you should have some happy and cheerful times ahead of you.

Brown
There is a real need for practicality and common sense, and you must avoid taking on more than you can logically deal with.

White
You will need to adapt to new situations and be cooperative and patient until you get the opportunity to make things work in your favour.

Grey
Someone, something or your general situation in life is not right, and this is undermining your health and your mental state. You need to move away from your current situation.

Black
This colour has two meanings. The first is a loss of some kind, but the second is of protection, so whatever is going on may make you sad, but it won't cause you a serious problem.

Silver
Your intuition is developing. Also, mother figures will be helpful.

Gold
Happiness and success are on the way; there may be a windfall, and father figures will be helpful.

Chapter Five:
Numerology and the Tarot

Every card has a number associated with it, and these numbers hold energy, but they also convey information. This book is not about numerology as such, but some primary data on the topic will benefit your readings.

Numerology is studied and used all around the world. While it has developed in different ways over time, the similarities in use suggest that they stem from one original source. Pythagoras believed each number has its own vibration and that the vibrations represented universal and divine realities reflected within our personalities and other aspects of life.

Each of the nine numbers reflects divine qualities in a precise way. The main numbers are 1 to 9 because, in numerology, double digits are added together to make a single number; for example, 5 and 4 are added together to make 9. Some systems use three of the doubled numbers, called Master Numbers, which are 11, 22 and 33.

Zero
There is not much written about Zero, other than that it was first used in India to signify nothing, but in the ninth century it became a number. Indeed, today we would be in trouble if it weren't considered a number, as all our computers run on Zero and One. From an esoteric perspective, it is thought to represent *perfection, wholeness, the ultimate*. For our purposes, we can consider it has a dual meaning, this being nothing or everything.

One
One is about new beginnings and the originating impulse behind any activity. It gives focus, initiative and a sense of direction. It is unique and it encompasses assertiveness and independence. It brings inspiration and strives to move forward. It denotes

5: Numerology and the Tarot

motivation, courage and leadership, which are the start of manifestation. It is one of the most optimistic numbers.

Two

Two is about union or the introduction of another element into the situation. It is also about duality. It is considered the womb from which all thoughts are nurtured, and it may also be related to the unconscious mind. Two can signify the need to balance opposing forces.

Three

Three expands the theme involved in the reading. In a relationship reading, it can indicate a third party being involved. Three is the generator that inspires our creative energy and motivates us into manifesting our innermost desires. Three is enthusiastic and optimistic.

Four

Four represents stability, hard work and perseverance, so it tells us that more effort may be needed to achieve our desired outcomes. Four is where the hard work gathers the thought processes of One with the emotion of Two and the creative energy of Three, which brings them into the physical world.

Five

Five is about travel, movement and changing circumstances that we may not want but which could be beneficial anyway. Five is the number of the reactionary. It hates to be held down, restricted or imprisoned, and thus gives expansion and demands change, freedom and independence to experience life to the full. Five often signifies struggle.

Six

Six is the number of peace and harmony, and a time when balance is restored. It can indicate success after the struggles of five. It is the number of the heart and the home, of family, security and love. Its principle is that of care, service, duty and responsibility.

Seven
Seven represents the wisdom seeker and the search for an inner truth. Not everything is exactly as it seems. Seven is introspective and it seeks perfection. Seven resonates with the attributes of spiritual awakening, and it wants to break free of any recurring patterns that make life difficult for us. Seven is a deeply mystical and spiritual number; it relates to a retreat into solitude, searching our souls and reaching into our hidden depths.

It appears that we may have our distant relatives to thank for numbers. With their relatively large brains, Neanderthals are credited with inventing language and art, and they were the first to count, or think in numbers. Around 38,000 BCE, one typical design found in rock art was a series of seven dots or parallel lines that are believed to have had sacred significance.

Eight
Eight is the number of success of expansion and opportunity. Some caution will be needed, with projects that are nearing completion. Eight is generous and warm-hearted, open, spontaneous, creative, outgoing, broad-minded, accepting and loving, confident, self-sufficient and self-sacrificing.

The number Eight seems to mean something to people all around the world, as we can see in the list below:

- In China, it represents harmony, prosperity and the cosmos.
- In Egypt, it is the number of Thoth - the wisdom keeper.
- In Greece, it represents Hermes - the God of sacred geometry.
- For the Romans, it represented freedom and equality.

5: Numerology and the Tarot

- To Buddhists, it means "completion of all possibilities" and the "Eight-Fold Path".
- To Hindus Eight by Eight is the order of the celestial world that is to be established on Earth.
- In Jewish tradition, Eight stands for perfect intelligence and splendour.
- To Christians, it symbolises regeneration, rebirth and the "beatitudes".
- To Muslims, Eight denotes the throne that encompasses the world, supported by eight angels, corresponding to the eight divisions of space and the groups of letters in the Arabic Alphabet.
- Spiritually, Eight is the goal of the initiate, having passed through the seven heavens. It is the number of paradise regained, regeneration, resurrection and perfect rhythm.
- There are eight winds, eight directions and eight spokes in the "wheel of time".
- There are eight notes in an octave.
- In the Tarot, the Major Arcana card numbered Eight is the Strength card. Hence, we connect to our inner strength, wisdom, vision and desire to expand spiritual consciousness, balance and harmony within ourselves and on earth. As we take responsibility for our thoughts, feelings and actions, the results we manifest in our lives and the world we live in, then so we create the clarity necessary to change.
- Eight is the number of karma, which is the spiritual law of cause and effect.
- Visually, Eight depicts the ancient saying "as above, so below", and when on its side, it mirrors the symbol for infinity.

Nine
Nine is about the end of a cycle that automatically incorporates rebirth. It represents endings and beginnings. It is about completing this current cycle's growth by reviewing our lives and letting go,

clearing the way for new beginnings on personal, national, and global levels. Nine stands for humanitarianism, compassion, philanthropy, idealism and tolerance. Nine is both self-sacrificing and self-sufficient in its march towards progress and the fulfilment of personal and collective vision. It holds the spiral of happy returns because all numbers multiplied by Nine always reduce to Nine, thus symbolising the return to the source.

Ten
When reaching this point in the Major Arcana of the Tarot, the card is the Wheel of Fortune, representing a turning point. Now we add the digits together so that Ten becomes One, thus starting a new cycle.

Eleven
Not only doubles the energy of number One but is also a karmic number which resonates with the energy of spiritual awakening and enlightenment. It enables us to overcome our limitations. Now we can connect to the divine influence within and without ourselves and live to our soul's full potential, thus changing our world for the better.

The Justice card is number Eleven, and as it is a master number, it stays eleven.

Chapter Six:
Symbolism

The Tarot is full of symbols; for instance, you probably have noticed the infinity symbol that appears on many cards. Its meaning is universal, but that is not the case with every symbol, because they can have different meanings in different cultures. In western cultures, owls usually mean wisdom, but an owl implies deception in Native American culture. Therefore, it is essential to interpret symbols for yourself.

The circle is believed to be the oldest known symbol on our planet because it is seen in cave drawings around the world. The circle initially represented the sun and moon, and these were revered by early civilisations. The circle is also the root of the modern symbol for the feminine. The equilateral cross and circle depict the horizon line as the sun moves from east to west, but in the Native North American culture, it means the four directions of the wind, while it also represents the four elements of earth, air, fire and water. The Chinese see the centre of the cross as the ether. It is also the symbol representing Melchisedec and the four archangels supporting the universe. The equilateral cross and circle has always been a very sacred symbol. Even now, this symbol has been adopted to represent the modern Neo-Nazi Party, just as Hitler took an ancient Tibetan symbol of healing and reversed it to make the Swastika.

    The Caduceus is a symbol that is often used to represent healing, and it is the symbol used by the General Medical Council. It depicts two snakes entwined around a rod and coming together at the top where there are two wings. The snakes cross at all the chakra points from the base to the third eye. The rod can represent the body, the snakes activate the chakras, the third eye opens to cosmic knowledge, and Kundalini climbs up the rod and out of the crown, forming a free spirit's wings. At any one time, we can be attracted to a different part of a symbol. One day it may be the wings and the idea of a free spirit, but it may be the snakes and the concept of shedding skins on another day. The rod may tell us we need to stand tall. If we look at the whole symbol, it could be interpreted as someone being a healer, while alternatively, it could mean a need for the strength of the rod, which encourages clients to shed what they no longer need and become free to soar and meet their full potential.

If you come across a shape or a symbol that you have never seen before, you can research it or ask others for their opinion, but in the end, it's what resonates with you that is important.

REVERSED CARDS

There are many schools of thought regarding cards that appear upside down in a spread. Most people feel this reverses the card's meaning, making a positive card negative and vice versa. Many Tarot readers deliberately reverse a dozen or so cards randomly while others take them as they come. Yet others ignore reverse meanings entirely and just turn the cards the correct way up. A reversed card could indicate blocked energy, internalised energy, too much or too little energy. Seeing the imagery upside-down may draw your eye to different symbols, but it could simply mean the

6: Symbolism

client needs to look at a situation from another perspective. Whether you choose to read reversed meanings or not is entirely up to you. I personally don't, but I will give a generalised meaning for reversed cards when I discuss the cards individually.

Many people worry about having a reading because they don't want to hear anything negative. In my experience, the cards don't foretell negative experiences. Still, they reveal the energy that can be found around a situation and allow us to become aware of these energies, enabling us to make informed decisions. Some Tarot readers ignore anything that looks negative and put a positive slant to their readings. None of these methods is "right" or "wrong", it all comes down to how you choose to read the cards.

Chapter Seven:
Introduction to the Major Arcana

The English Oxford dictionary definition of Arcana says, "secrets and mysteries" and this perfectly describes the energies of the Major Arcana. These twenty-two cards are the most important in the deck, and many readers only use these cards. I think this is limiting, but each to their own.

Each of the Major Arcana cards is also associated with different elements and different planets. The Major Arcana contains a fount of wisdom and imagery about our spiritual journey. The cards hold the key to the lessons we learn through life as we strive to gain enlightenment. The imagery contains symbols from all religious backgrounds both ancient and modern, so the more you learn and discover symbols and their meanings worldwide, the deeper and more meaningful your readings will be.

RITES OF PASSAGE

The journey taken by the Fool leads us through the twenty-one rites of passage that we all undertake. The Fool represents our soul's full potential, and the journey of life is an essential part of the evolution of both the psyche and the soul. We all pass from not knowing to knowing, and in time we become wiser due to our experiences. The cards may represent the figures we encounter along our journey and within the various stages, such as childhood, adolescence, mid-life and maturity. The first five cards can relate to the childhood phase, our inner spiritual guides and outer guides, parents and teachers.

THE FIRST FIVE CARDS

Magician, High Priestess, Empress, Emperor, Hierophant
Adolescence begins when the Fool starts to experience the conflicting forces within him as he tries to find his place in the world. This shows the adjustments made and the knowledge gained by experience, added to beliefs that have been picked up in childhood.

7: Introduction to the Major Arcana

In most decks, the Fool depicts a young man, but the Fool applies to us all, regardless of gender - as do all the cards that represent either male or female energy.

THE NEXT TWO CARDS
Lovers, Chariot
As the Fool begins the journey to maturity, he manages to link his personal experiences to the reality of his world. He starts to tame his ego, makes plans and takes action to achieve his ambitions through the tests and challenges the world affords him.

CARDS OF CONFLICT, COGITATION AND CHANGE
Strength, Hermit, Wheel of Fortune, Justice
As the Fool travels towards old age, he seeks his own individual identity through his knowledge and life experience. This is the midlife crisis stage, when he re-evaluates everything that he thought he knew, and he faces his inner truths. We often feel we face our own individual forty days and forty nights, lost in the wilderness.

CARDS OF CHALLENGE AND DIFFICULTY
Hanged Man, Temperance, Death, Devil, Tower
The Fool has some bad days, including experiencing trials and tribulations, loss, sadness and being tied to situations that do him no good. He gradually learns from these and moves forward again.

CARDS OF WISDOM AND OPTIMISM
Star, Moon, Sun
Finally, we overcome the darkness and re-enter the light.

THE FINAL CARDS
Judgement, The World
After the re-evaluation, the Fool realises that there are things he no longer needs. He can let go of everything, including old beliefs, thought patterns, people, careers and possessions, as he enters the final phase that brings rest, peace, renewed hope, faith and trust.

Chapter Eight:
The Major Arcana

This chapter offers interpretations covering the generally accepted meanings of the cards. However, a card reading's most valuable aspect is the meaning that each card has for you, especially if you take the time to meditate on the cards.

0 THE FOOL

Beginning, naivety

Many people place the Fool at the beginning of the deck, but some put it at the end because they don't consider zero a number. The Fool steps out into the unknown future with confidence and a sense of adventure. Perhaps he has come down from the mountain after a quest and is taking a leap of faith. He appears to be stepping off a ledge, and in many decks, he has his knapsack over his shoulder and a happy companion in the dog at his feet. The world seems to be his oyster.

We go through various cycles as we go through life, and they can be broken down into childhood, adolescence, adulthood and maturity. Another expression many religions often refer to is the Goddess's three faces: Maid, Mother and Crone. As we journey through life experiencing archetypal energies, we notice these cycles and continually move from one to the next. Hence there are constant new beginnings whereby we gain experience and wisdom. The Fool continues from one cycle to the next with his constant need to explore.

The feelings
Joy, freedom and courage.

The meaning
The beginning, a new cycle, youth, a leap of faith, being unaware of danger, inner wisdom beyond his years.

Planetary association
Uranus, which is concerned with awakening.

Element
Air.

In a reading
This card tells of the presence of joy, love and wisdom that has not yet been applied. The Fool is free from worldly concerns and perhaps oblivious to the prevailing circumstances. There are excitement and trepidation about what the future may hold. The client is ready for change, open to new ideas and new ways of being, and depending upon where they are in life, there will be a certain amount of wisdom that they are taking with them.

Reversed
The questioner may be underestimating a situation or acting carelessly, and not using inner wisdom.

Esoteric meaning
Searching for the meaning of life while assessed continuously and challenged as the questioner traverses his spiritual pathway without a care in the world.

Traditional Tarot In Focus

THE MAGICIAN

I THE MAGICIAN

Creativity in action
The Magician has all the tools he needs to create whatever he wishes, and most decks show these in the shape of a Cup, a Wand, a Pentacle and a Sword. He is smart and capable. He has one hand raised upward and one pointing down, representing his ability to take ideas and manifest them into reality. He is usually depicted with the infinity symbol over his head representing his connection to the divine. There is no magic here, just the Magician using his talents to transform his ideas and make them real.

The feelings
Control, power, taking charge of his own life and being creative.

The meaning
As above so below, good intentions and knowing he can manifest whatever he wants.

Planetary association
Mercury the messenger, who rules communication.

Element
Air.

8: The Major Arcana

In a reading
The questioner is focussed, confident and ready to achieve whatever they need. A time of creativity and purpose.

Reversed
The questioner may be in the clutch of their ego and misusing power for personal gain. They may be manipulating others or using a situation for their own ends.

Esoteric meaning
The need to continue taking the path towards enlightenment by connecting to natural energies and with the conscious use of thought, feelings, actions to manifest the divine qualities of love, wisdom and the "right" use of power.

Traditional Tarot In Focus

The High Priestess

II THE HIGH PRIESTESS

Secrets to be revealed
In many decks, the High Priestess sits on a throne. The Torah is on their lap, showing their connection to, and understanding of, universal law. In many decks, they sit between two pillars, one dark and one light; one is inscribed with the letter B representing Binah and the divine energy of the Mother Goddess, whilst the other letter J represents Jehovah, the divine face of God. I often see them as Buddha (mind) and Jesus (heart) and combine the two concepts; the Empress finds and shares peace, love and harmony via insight, balance and compassion.

The feelings
A very spiritual, intuitive, secure, private person who uses their intelligence to find their way forward.

The meaning
A guardian angel, fate to be revealed, secrets to be uncovered, looking to the future. This card represents the middle path between heart and mind.

8: The Major Arcana

Planetary association
The moon, which is eternally mysterious and which denotes intuition and compassion.

Element
Water.

In a reading
The questioner or someone close to them is wise enough to help the subject find the necessary path for a good outcome. The card indicates revelations, use of spiritual knowledge and unconscious feelings.

Reversed
The questioner is lost and not connecting to their deeper emotions. They are skirting the issues or perhaps avoiding them altogether.

Esoteric meaning
Conscious emotions can be used to transform the personality into the soul's natural compassionate nature.

III THE EMPRESS

Relating
The Empress represents the mother figure and fertility, with the cornfield that most cards show suggesting growth and a fertile harvest. If shown wearing a crown, this contains twelve stars, representing their connection to the signs and houses of the horoscope. Usually, there are myrtle leaves in the illustration, an ancient symbol showing that they have overcome their personal passions and are aware of the natural laws.

The feelings
The Empress listens to others and understands. They also create and represent beauty and harmony, financial abundance and emotional support. They suggest use of the right side of the brain.

The meaning
Growth, fertility, mother figure, marriage, good friendships.

Planetary association
Venus, the planet of abundance, love and beauty.

Element
Earth.

In a reading
Spiritual and emotional growth. Abundance abounds. Getting closer to others and partnerships of all kinds, bringing the opportunity to gain experience. It can even indicate marriage and parenthood.

Reversed
The questioner has become indecisive and perhaps confused about their direction. They may feel disconnected from themselves, or powerless.

Esoteric meaning
Creative self-expression through imagination.

IV THE EMPEROR

Authority
The Emperor is an older person who is usually shown sitting on a throne. They emit an air of confidence, power, order, authority and leadership. Just as the Empress represents the mother then so the Emperor represents the father. The throne may be shown decorated with the heads of rams, representing the sign of Aries.

The feelings
This is a dominant, stubborn authoritative person, but it also tells of personal will, even a protector, action, abundant energy and control.

The meaning
An authority figure, control, practical logic and possible rigidity.

Planetary association
Aries, which is ruled by Mars, the planet of personal will.

Element
Fire.

8: The Major Arcana

In a reading

The Emperor represents power and authority. Making decisions and moving forward. This character protects what belongs to them, but acts when necessary. Is this a time for protecting or for acting? It's a time to take back power and work with the knowledge and wisdom that has been gained over time.

Reversed

The questioner may be feeling tired, confused, and unable to see their way clearly or maybe worrying unduly.

Esoteric meaning

Tapping into the mind and manifesting the higher self.

V THE HIEROPHANT

Wisdom revealed
The Hierophant (sometimes called the Pope) may be shown on a throne and holding the papal symbol of crossed keys, representing the "keys to the kingdom" that correspond to the potential to unlock the soul's nature. Depending upon the deck, there are many possible symbols related to religion - especially, Christianity. They sit between two pillars representing the outer expression of our inner search for spiritual meaning.

The feelings
The Hierophant likes to be seen to be right, and while they are conservative, they see the need to make changes when past patterns no longer serve. They are searching for meaning.

The meaning
Contract, marriage, bringing things together, a spiritual person who may work for the church.

Planetary association
Venus, the planet of abundance, love and beauty.

8: The Major Arcana

Element
Earth.

In a reading
The questioner has reached a point in life where they are seeking greater meaning. The inner changes they make will reap the benefit, and outer changes will follow. Adjustments are occurring to accommodate the inner spiritual growth that is now taking place.

Reversed
The questioner is a slave to social norms, so they don't want to rock the boat by thinking for themselves, which may stunt their own spiritual growth. They fear being ostracised if they question their culture and the norms that inhibit their creativity.

Esoteric meaning
Using intuitive inner knowledge in daily life that comes from the higher self or soul.

Traditional Tarot In Focus

THE LOVERS

VI THE LOVERS

Union of opposites
Different cards offer different images, but most show a man and a woman, and sometimes also illustrations taken from the story of Adam and Eve. There may be an angel watching over the couple, or a Tree of Knowledge. The symbolism is about relationships and the benefits or problems they bring.

The feelings
Someone open-minded. The other person will help the questioner find a sense of unity within, bringing together their nature's masculine and feminine sides.

The meaning
Choices and decisions. Physical relationships; maybe a sexual obstacle.

Planetary association
Gemini, which is ruled by Mercury, the messenger.

Element
Air.

8: The Major Arcana

In a reading
There is either a person or a situation that is important to the questioner. Communication will be the key to success, but when the card is applied to the self, integration of various sides of the individual's nature through acceptance is the way forward.

Reversed
There are difficulties in a relationship caused by the lack of open and honest communication, either with oneself or others.

Esoteric meaning
Balancing opposites within the self and integrating all facets of the personality, ego, and soul; may be conscious or unconscious.

Traditional Tarot In Focus

VII The Chariot

Use of will
Most decks show the charioteer standing on their chariot with a sceptre in their hand, showing they are a high ranking official. Some symbols show that we are frequently faced with the paradox of life, but other symbols may suggest their ability to help us integrate the higher self and the ego. It shows the charioteer's depth of knowledge and wisdom.

The feelings
The will to accomplish personal goals, because the questioner can achieve anything they set out to do with discipline and focus.

The meaning
A crossroads, moving on and good luck.

Planetary association
Cancer, which is ruled by the moon.

Element
Water.

8: The Major Arcana

In a reading
The chariot represents inner will and the wisdom to accomplish goals by balancing physical, emotional, mental and spiritual needs. It also tells of overcoming obstacles.

Reversed
The questioner has problems, conflicting emotions and needs.

Esoteric meaning
Purely personal goals may be transformed or sacrificed for the greater good.

VIII STRENGTH

Personal power
This card indicates personal power. It usually depicts a young woman helping a lion. She shows no fear and is armed only with her compassion and desire to help. She represents the ability to overcome humanity's inherent animal nature using compassion, love and determination. She is likely to have the symbol of infinity about her head, indicating her connection to the higher realms.

The feelings
Correct use of personal power to overcome obstacles, and to overcome life's barriers. A test of the subject's ability to endure, producing a greater sense of self-confidence.

The meaning
Inner and outer strength, powerful emotions, keeping control, slightly egotistical and instinctual.

Planetary association
Leo and the Sun, the planet of the self.

8: The Major Arcana

Element
Fire.

In a reading
This shows the questioner dares to achieve anything if they do so from a place of love and compassion rather than one of force.

Reversed
This can indicate an abuse of personal power or indecisiveness over a situation. Clarification is needed.

Esoteric meaning
The correct use of personal power to transform baser nature and become the best one can be.

N.B: Some older forms of Tarot give the Strength card the number 11 and the Justice card the number 8. However, although the "old-style" images in this book reflect that idea, the interpretations I give here are the commonly used and understood number 8 for Strength and 11 for Justice.

THE HERMIT

IX THE HERMIT

Inner reflection
The hermit is usually depicted as a person walking alone with a lantern lighting the way, representing both the inner and outer search for deeper meaning. They are elderly, indicating they have searched long and hard, and they now stand at the top of a hill, which leads us to suppose they have reached their goal and gained wisdom along the way. They hold their lantern high so others might see the way as well.

The feelings
Wisdom and knowledge, a light at the end of a tunnel.

The meaning
This can be a card of past. It can show loneliness, but it also indicates the presence of a teacher who is wise and supportive. A lantern lights the way, so someone is coming to help, and it may mean someone is coming back from the past.

Planetary association
Virgo, ruled by Mercury, the planet of communication.

8: The Major Arcana

Element
Earth.

In a reading
The card suggests that the person needs a time of inner reflection to reach the light at the tunnel's end. There are probably misconceptions that need to be cleared away before they can see their way clearly. It can also indicate than an older, more experienced person will enter the subject's life in the role of a teacher who will assist them on their journey.

Reversed
Someone uses escapism as a tool to avoid releasing old, outdated belief patterns and patterns of behaviour that are holding him back.

Esoteric meaning
Reflection and soul-searching to bring about the integration of all facets of the personality.

Traditional Tarot In Focus

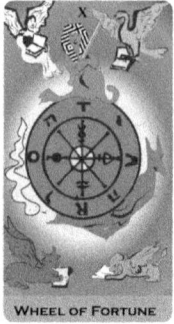
WHEEL OF FORTUNE

X THE WHEEL OF FORTUNE

Opportunities, chance, karma
Most decks show this card as a wheel, often with the word TAROT spelt out at the four directions, pointing to the wisdom in the cards. When read in reverse, they spell Tora, which relates to the first five books of the Old Testament, which give us the laws of righteous living and the Ten Commandments. They often show the four letters of the Hebrew alphabet depicting God's divine name, YHVH, indicating our connection to the divine knowledge. Depending upon the deck, there may be a host of other symbols, but most relate to knowledge and change.

The feelings
Life is a gift, change is inevitable, a surprise is coming, and the subject may be working hard and being rewarded by life.

The meaning
Opportunities will return.

Planetary association
Jupiter, the planet of expansion and luck.

8: The Major Arcana

Element
All the elements of fire, earth, air, water and spirit.

In a reading
This is a card of good luck because it indicates positive change and opportunities coming around once again. It suggests that the questioner should grasp the opportunity when it comes, and if nothing happens immediately, it will do so a bit later. Taking advantage of this opportunity will have positive effects on life.

Reversed
This card can mean bad luck, but as we know, every so-called bad experience teaches us something, and it always has a silver lining. So be aware that there will be some positive purpose.

Esoteric meaning
Becoming aware of the cycles of life which may be long, short, good or bad. The world keeps turning and every new day offers new opportunities. The waves will still be rolling up the beach, and with each wave, the beach will look slightly different. What comes around goes around.

XI Justice

Balance
On most decks, the scales of justice and the sword of truth are present, ensuring that justice is based on honesty, integrity and truth. This card is about balance, which may be between light and dark, good and bad, the laws of heaven and of earth or the soul and ego.

The feelings
Sense of justice, security and reaping what the individual sows, especially in relationships.

The meaning
Legal issues, balance, getting what is deserved, and the right side will win.

Planetary association
Venus, the goddess of beauty, but above all of harmony.

Element
Air.

8: The Major Arcana

In a reading
This card shows that the questioner will get what they deserve, whether good or bad, depending upon their karma. If someone has been fair, they will receive fairness, if they have been (or are being) totally absorbed in self-interest, they will reap what they have sown. If any legal actions are involved, the card implies that justice will be served.

Reversed
When reversed, this card indicates injustice, bias and prejudice, or perhaps decisions that have not been fully thought through and may be mistaken. Important decisions may need to be looked at carefully again. The questioner should try to be fair in all their dealings.

Esoteric meaning
The balancing aspect of the laws of cause and effect.

N.B: Some older forms of Tarot give the Strength card the number 11 and the Justice card the number 8. However, although the images in this book reflect that idea, the interpretations I give here are the commonly used and understood number 8 for Strength and 11 for Justice.

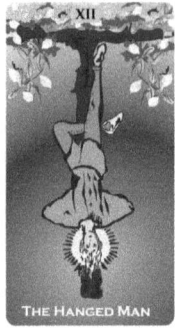

XII THE HANGED MAN

Sacrifice
When looking at this card, it becomes evident that the questioner should look at their situation from a different perspective. Something will have to go before they can move on. This could be a certain way of thinking or an outdated belief rather than an item or object of some kind. The Hanged Man is suspended from a tree that seems to have a lot of fruit on it, suggesting that if the questioner looks at things differently, the outcome would be fruitful. In some decks, if the card is reversed, it makes the shape of a number four, which is the number of manifestation.

The feelings
The subject does not like making decisions. A job is done, and it is time to reconsider the future. Sacrifice to achieve.

The meaning
Nothing is happening; look at things from a different perspective, make sacrifices, and have a different attitude to sexual matters.

Planetary association
Neptune, a visionary planet that seeks earthly change to enable

spiritual transformation.

Element
Water.

In a reading
This card says that something must go if the desired outcome is to be reached, and a change of perspective needs to be brought to bear.

Reversed
The card can signify someone who is being very selfish. Someone who may be pretending to let go but who has an ulterior motive, or who does not intend to do as they say they will.

Esoteric meaning
Reflection about oneself and the releasing of lower patterns of behaviour, thus attaining a higher spiritual perspective.

XIII Death

Transformation, endings and rebirth
This card immediately brings up people's fear of bad things and even physical death. This is not the case; this is a card of transformation through releasing and letting go of what is no longer needed.

The feelings
Endings and new beginnings, transformation, regeneration or loss.

The meaning
This card can mean the end of something, change or a new beginning. I also see this card representing an undertaker, a forensic scientist or someone who cares for the elderly.

Planetary association
Pluto, which transforms and renews.

Element
Earth.

8: The Major Arcana

In a reading
This card tells the questioner that something must end, and while this may be painful, it cannot be avoided if the way is to be cleared so that they can move forward afresh. It can be the loss of a relationship, a job or a belief, but this will lead to a better future.

Reversed
This means that someone is not prepared to let go; they fear change and will do anything to prevent it.

Esoteric meaning
This signifies the death of old disempowering beliefs, allowing a new golden age of spirituality to dawn for the subject.

XIV TEMPERANCE

Self-control and patience
In most decks, the central figure in the card is shown as an angel. The angel is an androgynous being who denotes the fusion between the male and female energies, while the halo shows that divine spirit is overseeing the questioner and their situation. The being has one foot on land and one in water, indicating the need for balance between practical action, emotions and intuition. Angels are God's messengers, and as such, suggest that the subject should see the situation through the eyes of love and compassion before making any rash decisions. Remember all things happen in divine time.

The feelings
Healing, things happening slowly, but there is no need to force the pace because the desired outcome will happen in divine time. Be patient.

The meaning
Moderation, overseas travel, foreigners, mixed relationships, enjoyment of partying and entertainments.

8: The Major Arcana

Planetary association
Jupiter, the planet of good luck and of reconciling opposites.

Element
Fire.

In a reading
This card advises the subject to take their time. All things happen for a reason and in divine time, not just when they want it to. The questioner should relax and go with the flow, and all will be well.

Reversed
When reversed, this card could mean that the questioner is very impatient and will make rash decisions, which will need to be reversed if their goal is to be achieved. The old adage "more haste less speed" is appropriate here.

Esoteric meaning
By probing the unconscious and using mindful self-control and temperance, the ego-personality will integrate with the soul energy and become whole.

XV THE DEVIL

Order versus chaos
At first glance, this card conjures up images of evil, destruction and death. The inverted pentagram at the devil's head tells us that mankind is at the mercy of their baser emotions and is separated from their connection to the divine. If you look closely at the card, it is like The Lovers card, which is number six. The differences are that the two characters on the card are usually shown chained to the pillar upon which the devil sits, suggesting that their desires are holding them back. Interestingly, the card is numbered fifteen, which in numerology reduces to a six, which means peace, harmony and success. Therefore, the card shows us it is within each person to overcome the things holding them back.

The feelings
The person is already chained. There is bondage, unfulfilled desires, egocentric ideas, being trapped in a situation that inhibits growth. The current situation is harmful, and it may be controlled by someone selfish.

The meaning
Material greed is present as are lust and temptation. A card of addictions and abuse, promiscuity, adultery and deceit.

8: The Major Arcana

Planetary association
Saturn, which shows the way.

Element
Earth.

In a reading
This card is often about control, so the individual may be controlling themselves or controlling others for personal gain. It is also about giving away personal power, perhaps to gain a hollow victory that will not be good for them or others. They may be controlled by others to their own detriment. Nothing good can come of this situation until they find the light within to break free. It also means manipulation and abuse.

Reversed
This means the subject has broken free or is about to. A new order will come from the chaos they have been experiencing, and they have reached the light at the end of the tunnel.

Esoteric meaning
It is time to break free from the ego's selfish desires and transform them into the charitable purpose of the higher-self and soul, thus "living with soul" every day of the subject's life. Evil spelt backwards is Live, so when the questioner releases themselves from their selfish desires, they begin to live the life they were born to live.

Traditional Tarot In Focus

XVI THE TOWER

Destruction
In most decks, the tower is hit by lightning, indicating that something will come to a sudden end. This can mean a job, a relationship or even a home, but the bricks will still be standing, so the questioner still has the knowledge and skills needed to build a better and more practical future.

The feelings
This can predict a rocky patch, sudden outbursts of anger and impatience, foundations no longer serving the highest good, a struggle to gain greater awareness, looking at the bigger picture. Change for the better.

The meaning
Sudden happenings, arguments.

Planetary association
Mars, the God of War.

Element
Fire.

8: The Major Arcana

In a reading
This card means that something within the questioner's life has been built on shaky ground or misunderstandings. When we get what we think we want, we may realize we were mistaken, and that those things don't make us happy. It also indicates that although this process cannot be avoided; there will be a better, more stable future.

Reversed
There will still be setbacks, but they will not be as tricky as they might have been.

Esoteric meaning
Lightning (spirit) is striking the individual's ego (Tower), enabling new understanding and meaning to grow within them, allowing them to make improvements.

XVII THE STAR

Revelation and healing
This card usually shows a person by a pool (which denotes the universal consciousness) while pouring water and watching the ripples going out. There are traditionally seven other eight-pointed stars on the card, representing the eight-fold path of Buddha. Alternatively, this can be seen as seven stars, representing the seven main chakras of the body, which can be healed and balanced to create the eighth star, placed above the figure's head, indicating a connection to the divine. The Star is numbered seventeen, which equals eight in numerology, meaning expansion, opportunity and eternity.

The feelings
Testing new waters, inspiration from above, inner strength and spiritual guidance.

The meaning
Wishes will come true, being strong and healthy. Intelligence and insight needed for success.

Planetary association
Uranus the awakener.

Element
Air.

In a reading
This card indicates creativity and healing. The questioner will be successful, not only on the temporal plane but also in the spiritual.

Reversed
There is a lack of clarity regarding the direction of the subject's life. There needs to be meditation and reflection on what is important to him so he can find a new direction. They shouldn't lose hope, because all will be well.

Esoteric meaning
The search for spiritual enlightenment and wisdom.

XVIII THE MOON

Psychic awareness, illusion and danger
The moon has no light of its own, because it is merely reflecting the light of the sun, so it suggests that the subject's emotional nature is eclipsing their spiritual connection. In many decks, various strange animals appear, implying a pathway to enlightenment, but there are things the subject should avoid. They may even wish to avoid the path altogether. Numerology reduces the number eighteen to a nine denoting that something is working its way to an end, which inevitably creates a new beginning.

The feelings
The individual should be aware of what is going on around them, and should follow their instincts. There may be self-deception or hidden forces at work, beware.

The meaning
Things can be deceptive. The questioner may have their head in the sand. Some things are hidden. Sadness, deep emotions, a need to think clearly and mountains to climb.

8: The Major Arcana

Planetary association
Jupiter, planet of good luck and Neptune, planet of the visionary.

Element
Water.

In a reading
Beware, all is not as it seems. The subject should take their head out of the sand and look at the situation objectively. Are people lying to them, or are they deluding themselves? Either way, they should trust in their intuition to guide them and not allow their imagination to run away with them.

Reversed
Time to balance emotions with reason. Things are not as difficult as they appear.

Esoteric meaning
Time to develop intuition and psychic ability that will assist the questioner in connecting to the divine dwelling within them.

Traditional Tarot In Focus

XIX The Sun

Fulfilment
This is a happy card because the sun is shining down, and all is well. This card is often depicted with a child on a horse out exploring the world, and there may be a wall behind the child, indicating that hard work is behind the questioner and there is only joy and exploration ahead. The child is free to use its own experience, knowledge, wisdom and intuition on the next stage of its journey.

The feelings
Happiness and contentment. Things are going well; gifts and opportunities are being offered.

The meaning
Happiness and success, happy family life and growth.

Planetary association
The Sun, which gives us life.

Element
Fire.

8: The Major Arcana

In a reading

The individual has achieved a lot, but now they are entering a period of expansion. They have wisdom and knowledge from experience, so they are well equipped for this time of joy and exploration.

Reversed

The questioner is avoiding moving forward into the future.

Esoteric meaning

The needs and desires of the ego-personality have been transcended. The road to enlightenment is open.

Traditional Tarot In Focus

XX Judgement

Beginnings and rebirth
In most decks, an angel sounds a trumpet and breathes fire into the dead, thus resurrecting and breathing new life into a person or situation. There may be a man, representing male energy and the conscious mind, a woman, expressing female energy, intuition and the emotions, and the child, representing integration and new life.

The feelings
Self-understanding has been reached, and a new phase of life is about to begin.

The meaning
Rebirth. Life changes for the better. A crossroads, but also travel abroad.

Planetary association
Pluto, the planet of transformation and renewal.

Element
The ether.

In a reading
This is a time of new beginnings, utilizing everything that has been learned so far. It is an exciting time where everything is possible.

Reversed
The questioner needs to let go of the past and embrace the unknown.

Esoteric meaning
Fear and self-doubt have been overcome, and the individual is free to explore their spiritual connection to the divine. The road to enlightenment has been reached.

XXI THE WORLD

Mastery
The World represents, completion, victory over obstacles, freedom and infinite potential, so this card means the "world is the subject's oyster". They have overcome all the challenges and are now ready to embark upon the next adventure.

The feelings
There is a sense of self-esteem that has been developed by the process of inner and outer growth. Recognition from others is likely.

The meaning
Personal success, potential fulfilled, encompasses everything. The sky is the limit, international travel.

Planetary association
Saturn, the planet that shows the way.

Element
Ether.

8: The Major Arcana

In a reading
This card shows that the individual has achieved their goals through hard work and perseverance, and they have gained the necessary experience needed to move on. Their self-esteem is high, and they have been acclaimed by others.

Reversed
The questioner may feel blocked, they he may have low self-esteem. They are in a period of stagnation and lack of motivation. They don't appreciate themselves or their talents.

Esoteric meaning
Freedom and a time to share and teach what has been learned.

And Remember…
As you learn and expand your knowledge, you will develop your views and interpretations of each card. The meanings given here are the accepted meanings of the cards. As you progress, you will hear other readers' opinions and perhaps experience the cards differently within your own life. You will intuit new meanings for different people as you start to do readings. At the end of the day, it is what a card means to you that is important, and if you are reading the card intuitively, you will recognise what it means for each individual client, rather than giving a general meaning to everyone you read for.

Chapter Nine:
The Minor Arcana

The Minor Arcana is split into four suits, each containing Ace through to Ten, plus four Court cards: The Page, Knight, Queen and King. The Major Arcana represents archetypes and aspects of our spiritual journey, but so do the Minor Arcana cards in their own ways. Each suit represents different areas of our lives, and it characterises spiritual growth that evolves from our mental, emotional and physical selves.

First, an idea pops into our mind (thoughts), if it feels good (emotions), we act on it and bring something into physical reality. Therefore, Swords relate to thoughts, Cups denote feelings and emotions, Wands tell of actions, and Pentacles signify results. The cards of the Minor Arcana bring these themes down from the spiritual realm into the practical world, to show how these aspects operate in daily life, and they can also be used to give an indication of timing.

~~~ SWORDS ~~~

Swords are the suit of mental activity, thought and reason, rational thinking, decisions and intellectual pursuits. Most of the struggles in our lives can be laid at the door of our thoughts. Many people spend days agonizing over decisions due to the fear of "getting it wrong" or worrying about "what might happen". In other words, our fears are in our minds and our imaginations.

Swords are concerned with the ideals of justice, truth and ethical principles. In most decks in this suit, one finds several negative cards depicting nightmares, craftiness, pain and restriction. Our rational mind is a precious asset because it is an accumulation of our experience and everything we have learned in this lifetime. Still, it is also an aspect of the ego, so it can lead us astray if it is not infused with the wisdom that comes from our higher selves.

9: The Minor Arcana

Human Aspect	Thoughts & Imagination
Element	Air
Direction	West
Season	Autumn
Timing	Years

This emphasis on the mentality is related to the masculinity within us all.

To get a closer connection to the suit of Swords, think, feel and sense the element of air and how it changes. For example, what does a light breeze feel like? Or how about a howling gale, dampness, dryness, warmth or cold. Focus on the air in your body. The breath, the lungs and the gases created within the body. What are the cleansing qualities of air? What elements combine to make the air that we breathe, which are invisible but present? What if there was no air? How have we as a species harnessed air for our own good?

Meditation for the element of air
Play some relaxing music and meditate on the element of air, and on thoughts and imagination, the west, autumn, and years going by, and see what you experience.

Ace of Swords

Principle
Victory.

Feelings
New ideas, cut away, innovative.

Meaning
Beginnings, great force.

In a reading
This card symbolises new ideas, inspiration, success and intellectual accomplishment. Take a new idea and run with it because victory is in sight. Perhaps this is a double-edged sword, and the subject needs to cut away from the past or past ideas to achieve a successful future. It is a card of new beginnings, and it foretells a quest for total truth.

Reversed
The card tells us there are confusion, powerlessness and an overactive imagination. Someone is being threatened, and there may be destruction and the misuse of power.

Two of Swords

Principle
An alliance or friendship may not be what it seems.

Feelings
Indecisiveness, the questioner won't face life, afraid, timid.

Meaning
The individual is turning their back on their emotions and intuition, refusing to see stalemate.

In a reading
Turning a blind eye, a stalemate has been reached and the situation needs to be looked at again, this time using intuition and noticing how things feel. Someone is being very indecisive, and sometimes it is better to think about what one would regret not doing rather than what should be done.

Reversed
The card speaks of treachery, violence, wilful misguidance and misleading advice, either given or taken, as well as trickery and deceit.

THREE OF SWORDS

Principle
Disintegration.

Feelings
Highly emotional, anxious, in despair.

Meaning
Heartbreak, loss, karma healing the past, present and future.

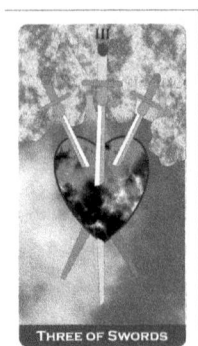

In a reading
On one level this is obviously about heartbreak, pain and loss. It also means we can use this destruction to achieve a positive end because it symbolizes that something obsolete will be cleared away to make room for something better to come. On another level, it is about karma; so, a past life pattern is being presented, enabling the questioner to grow spiritually and to heal the situation across past, present and future lifetimes.

Reversed
The subject is in denial about a situation or loss, thus ensuring the pain continues. It can also indicate mental and psychological disorders.

9: The Minor Arcana

FOUR OF SWORDS

Principle
Rest.

Feelings
Tired, resting, inactive, lazy or depressed.

Meaning
Rest and recuperation, strength in reserve, time-out.

In a reading
The person needs to rest because life has been difficult. Much has been overcome, but this is the time to rest for a while and then gather energy to complete the last part of the task. The card suggests someone is suppressing their feelings. Still, when the feelings are released, the energy being used to suppress those emotions will be released, which will enable the subject to regain his strength and move forward.

Reversed
This card may indicate a short illness or temporary problems.

Five of Swords

Principle
Defeat.

Feelings
The questioner must watch his back.

Meaning
Mental struggle, bullying, being victimised, a battle of wits or mental defeat.

Five of Swords

In a reading
This represents loss, failure, dishonour, a need to curb futile belligerence, accept the inevitable, and swallow one's pride. It speaks of negative attitudes and thoughts. It can also mean it is time to cut losses and move on, taking note of what has been achieved to date, and therefore live to fight another day.
It can also mean you won, you have made your point, walk away, no need to look over your shoulder anymore.

Reversed
The subject will be cleared and vindicated of any misunderstanding, blame or gossip. The enemy will be revealed as a vicious troublemaker. This can also indicate conflict that, however often the individual walks away from it, continues to follow him.

Six of Swords

Principle
A journey.

Feelings
Calm, organised, although things have not been easy. Moving to a calmer period in life.

Meaning
Stormy seas but things are getting better and maybe someone coming to help and showing the questioner they are not alone. Overseas travel is possible soon.

In a reading
Things have not been easy, but the individual will be moving into calmer waters and they will not be doing it alone.

Reversed
There is no quick way out of present difficulties. A planned trip is postponed. It also implies when one obstacle is overcome, there may yet be others.

Seven of Swords

SEVEN OF SWORDS

Principle
Possibilities.

Feelings
Self-restrictions, own worst enemy, does not face up to things, changeable but also streetwise.

Meaning
Sneaky, changing the mind, stealing, underhandedness, a one-sided relationship, still work to be done.

In a reading
It is time to think about changing direction. The individual has not failed, and there is a lot they are taking with them, so it's probably best to cut and run. Beware of treachery.

Reversed
Any losses will be returned and wishes will be fulfilled. The time has come to take decisive action.

EIGHT OF SWORDS

Principle
Temporary crisis.

Feelings
Being trapped.

Meaning
Mental processes are restricting, not facing the truth of a situation. The subject says they can't or won't?

In a reading
The restrictions the person is feeling are brought about by their thought processes, some of which may be genuine reasons, while others may be excuses, but there are Swords in reach on the card so a new way of thinking will remove the restrictions. The subject may have been incarcerated or excluded in some way.

Reversed
The questioner needs to free themselves from some of the limiting factors of the past. There are skeletons in the closet that need clearing out so they can allow themselves to let go of old patterns of behaviour and belief systems that have held them back. They must forget about being the victim.

Nine of Swords

Principle
Despair.

Feelings
Fear, sorrow, paranoia.

Meaning
Metal anguish, nightmares, torment, grief-stricken.

In a reading
The subject is in deep sorrow and may be paralyzed by fear. If depressed, they need to seek help to release their emotions and to heal. If fearful, they could be allowing their imagination to run away with them. The questioner must look at the fears realistically, make contingency plans and then work out what they want to happen and take the necessary steps to achieve it.

Reversed
There are worries, but they aren't too severe, and to some extent, the individual may be worrying unnecessarily.

TEN OF SWORDS

Principle
Ruin.

Feelings
Ending, loss, victim, suicidal tendencies.

Meaning
Stabbed in the back, loss, ending.

In a reading
Someone has it in for the questioner, and they must beware of being stabbed in the back. Something needs to end, especially any old, outdated, negative ways of thinking. A new outlook needs to be brought into being. This will take time and practice, but it can be done. Killing off old values and beliefs that no longer serve their purpose creates the opportunity for new beginnings in all areas of life.

~~~ Cups or Chalices ~~~

Cups are associated with our unconscious feelings, our emotions, our relationship with ourselves and others, in addition to our intuitive and psychic abilities and our spiritual experience. They describe inner states, feelings and relationship patterns. Most decks try to convey emotions in this suit; therefore, happiness, love, boredom, disappointment, confusion and dejection are usually represented and easily identified.

Human Aspect	Feelings & Emotions
Element	Water
Direction	East
Season	Summer
Timing	Days

To get a closer connection to the suit of Cups, think, feel and sense, the element of water. Consider the difference between the sea, rivers, lakes, ponds, rain, steam, snow and ice. Our bodies consist of eighty per cent water. Water represents our emotions, our feelings, how they change and manifest within our bodies, and the way feelings are influenced by other elements - by our thoughts, for instance?

Listen to the different sounds of water and notice how they make you feel. What if there was no water? How have we as a species harnessed water for our own good? Play some relaxing music and meditate on the element of water, the east, summer and days to see what you experience.

9: The Minor Arcana

ACE OF CUPS

Principle
Fertility and celebration.

Feelings
New life, giving, immaturity, naiveté, needing attention.

Meaning
A new emotional beginning.

In a reading
A new emotional beginning is being offered; a new life is in the making if this opportunity is seized. All is going to be well. The beginning of good things, whether they be love, joy, beauty or health or a new spiritual understanding. It is a card of faithfulness and all the positives of the unconscious mind.

Reversed
This card symbolizes a time of emptiness, especially emotionally. Cut off from our heart and have lost faith in love, emotionally drained.

Two of Cups

Principle
Love, union, partnerships.

Feelings
Enjoying partnerships, sharing, keeping thing simple, and innocence.

Meaning
Happy relationships, happy couple, friendship, romance, engagement, care.

In a reading
A new friendship, romance or partnership will begin with the chance for love and affection. There will be affinity, sympathy or joyous harmony with another. Reconciliation of opposites who now trust each other. Resolution of differences between people, and the integration of the internal energy.

Reversed
A need for understanding, humour and equality in a relationship. The love one feels for another is not returned. It can also represent quarrels.

Three of Cups

Principle
Success and celebration.

Feelings
Likes to party, anything for a laugh, talent, entertainment.

Meaning
Celebration and joy, close friends and family.

In a reading
A celebration in the offing. It is a card of abundance and happiness, so success is assured, especially around emotional issues.

Reversed
Self-indulgence to excess by the questioner or someone close to them

Four of Cups

Principle
Pause.

Feelings
Boredom and feeling sorry for oneself never satisfied, apathetic, lazy, refusing an opportunity.

Meaning
Self-pity, the questioner could miss an opportunity, wanting more, indifference, stuck in an emotional rut. Maybe the grass is greener on the other side.

In a reading
An opportunity is being offered, but the questioner is reluctant. They don't want to get involved, turning inward. They need to look at the experiences they have had and follow their heart by grabbing the Cup that is being offered. It is the silver lining from the cloud that will make it all worthwhile.

Reversed
A new relationship is possible. There is a desire to drink deeply from the cup of life and to celebrate. The subject needs to be careful not to over-indulge.

9: The Minor Arcana

FIVE OF CUPS

Principle
Disappointment in the past.

Feelings
Negative, easily upset, always disappointed, sad, pessimistic.

Meaning
Partial loss, things are not as bad as they seem, something coming, disappointment.

In a reading
Things have not been easy and there may be sadness and disappointment, but not all is lost. The individual should review the past and see what has been experienced and achieved. Take the good things forward and leave the rest behind.

Reversed
Shows recovery from regret and an acceptance of the past. The questioner realizes the full implications of the past and appreciates the lessons learned from the experience.

Six of Cups

Six of Cups

Principle
Pleasure from the past.

Feelings
Nostalgic, joys (or not) of childhood, living in the past, Victorian attitudes.

Meaning
Past, good old times, bad times, gifts and charity, reconciliation.

In a reading
The questioner may be a bit nostalgic, there may be memories arising from childhood that need to be released, what and why don't matter, because what matters is letting the bad memories go and keeping the good ones. Forgiveness for any poor misguided souls who may have hurt the subject, perhaps because they didn't know any better at the time and move one. The subject should also forgive themselves.

Reversed
Holding onto the past in an unhealthy way; living in the past and feeling sorry for themselves.

SEVEN OF CUPS

Principle
Imagination, reflection.

Feelings
Easily led, addictive, go with the flow, longing.

Meaning
Scattered focus, emotional confusion, getting things into perspective.

In a reading
This card talks of emotional confusion about those things that are important to the questioner. They seem to be somewhat mixed up not knowing what they feel or want. Their desires and needs may be conflicting. Everything feels chaotic, but from chaos comes a new order. They need to let go and allow the new order to materialise.

Reversed
This card can mean the subject is looking at the world through rose coloured glasses and ignoring the chaos of their emotions or that their actions are causing others.

Traditional Tarot In Focus

EIGHT OF CUPS

Principle
Concern, lack of confidence.

Feelings
Disappointment, having enough, the courage needed to leave a situation.

Meaning
Dissatisfied, time to move on and walk away.

In a reading
It is a card indicating retreat, withdrawal, self-pity, over-generosity and over-extending. The subject hesitates, and needs to think more positively; they are fed-up and dissatisfied. This card suggests that the subject requires a new path in life and starts to look for one. They shouldn't be afraid to leave the past behind, because there's much more in the world to see. They shouldn't be disillusioned because the future promises to be brighter. They should follow their heart and do what needs to be done. They may be dissatisfied with their accomplishments, so they need to take a break and make a change.

Reversed
Someone has abandoned something well-established for an impossible dream. It can imply the person is reckless and restless.

NINE OF CUPS

Principle
Achievement.

Feelings
Contentment, satisfaction.

Meaning
Happiness and contentment, getting what the questioner wants.

In a reading
This card indicates good health and much success. Nines represent personal integrity and completion of the final stage of development. The card represents triumph, victory and financial well-being. This card also signals enjoyment of good personal relationships, love and friendship. This is an omen for an assured future. It indicates the person will have satisfaction, contentment and physical well-being. It also is an indication of overcoming difficulties. It tells of emotional stability and a safe outlook. This person's inner being is so secure that it radiates in their aura in the form of good-will. Of course, being content is a lovely place to be, but more can be done; it is but a short step to joy.

Reversed
This can indicate a tendency to be over-sentimental and overlook others' faults, making the subject vulnerable to being used and abused for their hospitality. Kindness is taken for weakness. It can also be read as someone who is overly indulgent.

TEN OF CUPS

Principle
Peace, domestic happiness.

Feelings
Emotionally content, self-satisfied, selfish, always wants more, smug or vain.

Meaning
Pure joy and happiness, being free at last, children and happy families.

TEN OF CUPS

In a reading
This card signals peace, domestic happiness, wholeness, completion, optimism and successful development. Friendship, companionship and family happiness that will last. Fun group activities. Everything will work out for the best. Happy endings. This card tells of lasting happiness and security.

Reversed
This signals either a family quarrel or a loss of friendship and even a chance of betrayal. Young people may turn against their parents. It tells us that someone is manipulating society for personal gain.

9: The Minor Arcana

~~~ Wands (Rods, Staves, Batons) ~~~

This is the suit of creativity, action, movement, communication, spiritual and self-development. The Wands represent our day to day lives, but the suit also tells of travel. Action and energy are two keywords to this suit. In most decks, many of the cards show some type of activity or someone who appears to be enjoying the results of their efforts.

Human Aspect	Action, Behaviour
Element	Fire
Direction	South
Season	Spring
Timing	Weeks

To get a closer connection to the suit of Wands, think, see, sense, feel the energy of fire. It's destructive but also cleansing, and it could bring renewal. Again, what kind of fires can exist – candles, forest fires? How have we harnessed fire? What happens when we add fire to water or air?

Focus on the fire energy in your body. Where do we get our energy from? The food we eat creates the energy we need. We think we created fire and used it for ourselves, but fire was there long before we were, owing to lightning and the sun. How has our species harnessed fire for our own good? Play some relaxing music and meditate on the element of fire, the south, spring and weeks to see what you experience.

Traditional Tarot In Focus

ACE OF WANDS

Principle
Beginnings.

Feelings
A fresh start.

Meaning
A new job opportunity or venture, growth, ambition.

In a reading
A new job, career or enterprise is in the air, which could be the starting point of a new venture and the foundation for future successes. If the person uses their intuition well, fertility and conception are possible. This is a card of maturity and of artistic innovation.

Reversed
Setbacks in a new endeavour or over-confidence that could end in tears.

TWO OF WANDS

Principle
Obstacles.

Feelings
Choices, being outward-looking, contemplation from a safe-place, long-term goals, not a risk-taker.

Meaning
Waiting for the right time to come.

In a reading
Union and joining of opposing forces. Clarity, the spark of inspiration into an idea that can lead to something useful. The questioner has the means but is leaving things until the right day comes along. However, this starts today, so the card says the person needs to take some action to make their dreams come true.

Reversed
Loss of faith in their ideas and themselves. It can indicate a fear of success or a lack of progress due to refusing to act.

THREE OF WANDS

THREE OF WANDS

Principle
Successful enterprise.

Feelings
Restless, easily bored, needs support, the formation of enterprise and teamwork.

Meaning
Journeys and travel, trading and reaping the rewards.

In a reading
Tells the questioner that now is the time to go ahead with confidence. Being encouraged to move fearlessly into new areas. Patience will ensure obstacles are overcome. Creative enterprise, courage and initiative will be rewarded.

Reversed
Time for a reality check; are things likely to become too big to manage? Assess the practical implications of the situation.

FOUR OF WANDS

Principle
Relaxation.

Feelings
Joy and celebration, marriage.

Meaning
House and prosperity, material stability, marriage, house moves.

In a reading
Take time off and enjoy life, celebrate with family and friends. If the subject wants to move to a new house, the time is now. If not, then perhaps some redecoration.

Reversed
The individual should be careful about what they wish for; it may not be what they thought.

Traditional Tarot In Focus

FIVE OF WANDS

Principle
Strife.

Feelings
Argumentative, a challenging person who won't back down.

Meaning
Struggle, competition, challenging, others causing problems.

In a reading
There are struggles ahead, but success is assured in the long term. The questioner needs to look at their own behaviour and see if there are changes that they can make to ensure better working relations.

Reversed
Deception and dishonesty may be involved.

SIX OF WANDS

Principle
Excellent news, success.

Feelings
Winner, a genuine person, courageous, does not like failure, thrives on success.

Meaning
Victory, movement, travel.

SIX OF WANDS

In a reading
Hard work and patience have brought success, so take a lap of honour.

Reversed
Things are not going too well, and the subject will need to readdress the situation. He mustn't hold back if he wishes to succeed.

SEVEN OF WANDS

Principle
Valour.

Feelings
Creative, improvise, flexible, open-minded.

Meaning
Being on top of a situation, don't hold back, take a stand.

In a reading
The individual is staying on top of things, and although it may be demanding, they can achieve their goal. They may also be trying to do too much, which may be overpowering them. By stepping back a little, they can allow things to develop in their own good time.

Reversed
This can indicate loss through hesitation or giving up when the end is in sight.

EIGHT OF WANDS

Principle
Activation.

EIGHT OF WANDS

Feelings
Restlessness, being an ambitious person, always moving, happiness.

Meaning
Good news or job offers to come quickly, air travel or love coming the questioner's way.

In a reading
Job opportunities await, and one or two may involve travel. This card is about creativity in action, so it is time to take advantage of the incoming opportunities. It is also known as the "arrows of love"; therefore, if the individual is seeking a relationship, one or two offers could be on the way.

Reversed
Impulsiveness may lead to disaster.

NINE OF WANDS

Principle
Stability.

Feelings
Fed up, stubborn, defensive and resistance to change.

Meaning
Very protective through perseverance.

In a reading
This person can be very stubborn, but it may just as easily be someone else who is being stubborn. The subject needs to understand that others don't necessarily see things the way they do, and they don't want to do things the way the questioner thinks they should. Respecting each other's differences is the way forward. The subject should look at what has been achieved and perhaps take a short rest before going further.

Reversed
Perhaps the questioner has been waiting too long and has been too patient, so it is time to get moving again.

Ten of Wands

Principle
Oppression.

Feelings
Tired, burdened, and fed up, tenacity, endurance.

Meaning
Burdened, doggedly doing it all oneself.

In a reading
The end is in sight, but the questioner is worn out. They may be overburdened due to taking other people and their issues on board. If they can put some of their burdens down, they will complete their journey more easily. Others may be envious or jealous, and this may be causing a problem.

Reversed
There are social and financial difficulties that need to be sorted out.

Traditional Tarot In Focus

~~~ PENTACLES (COINS) ~~~

Pentacles represent abundance in all its forms. The suit is associated with work, career, the arts and crafts, self-employment, money, resources, learning, large organisations, results and the physical body. In most decks, we see craftsmen at work, business being conducted, the comfort and security of material wealth and the physical discomfort of shortage. Pentacles are the suit of practicality, security and worldly concerns, celebrating the beauty and abundance of nature, achievements, which we are in the physical world and our spiritual nature.

This suit is called Pentacles because, in many decks, each coin is shown with a pentacle on it. Other decks call this suit Coins.

HUMAN ASPECT	ACHIEVEMENT, MANIFESTATION
ELEMENT	EARTH
DIRECTION	NORTH
SEASON	WINTER
TIMING	MONTHS

To get a closer connection to the suit of Pentacles you need to think, feel and sense, the element of earth and how it changes, or is made up of soft sand, rock, clay and mud. Focus on your body. You are made up of so many different elements. You are manifestation. Where would we be without earth? What elements make up our planet and our earth? What if there was no earth, only rock or mud? How have we as a species harnessed earth for our own good? How does the sum total of your thoughts, feelings, and actions manifest itself in your physical life? What have you achieved, and what do you still want to become? Play some relaxing music and meditate on the element of earth, achievements, the north, winter and months, to see what you experience.

9: The Minor Arcana

ACE OF PENTACLES

Principle
New enterprise, success.

Feelings
Opportunist, lively, gifted, has potential.

Meaning
New financial opportunity.

In a reading
The suit indicates new energy and a revitalized interest in the material or financial areas of life. It may represent the beginning of new investments or the willingness to undertake a new business venture. It can indicate a career change.

Reversed
If any new financial opportunities are offered, take care because it isn't what it seems.

Two of Pentacles

Principle
Harmony during a time of change.

Feelings
Muddled, confused, indecisive, endless choices.

Meaning
Borrowing from Peter to pay Paul, hopping from one situation to another, being unfocused and not knowing what to do first. Opportunities will soon return.

In a reading
The person may be so busy juggling various aspects of their life that they are unaware of the new opportunities around them. There may be choices to make, but they can be changed if they don't work out well. Something or someone will return and help the subject to do what is most important to them.

Reversed
The questioner is trying to hold onto everything, but something needs to go if they are going to continue.

9: The Minor Arcana

THREE OF PENTACLES

THREE OF PENTACLES

Principle
Skill.

Feelings
Committed, conforms, and works well with others, no ambition, and a follower who lacks initiative.

Meaning
A card of employment, large buildings, corporations, working their way up in the workplace, a place of learning.

In a reading
A situation requires new learning, perhaps a course or workshop. This will lead to a more lucrative job and role in life, probably within a large organization. If the individual is self-employed, their company will expand.

Reversed
The subject (or someone around them) has not found a direction in life, so either they are still searching or don't have a clear idea of what they want. They aren't living up to their potential.

Four of Pentacles

Principle
Stability.

Feelings
Possessive, secretive, holds onto everything, insecure, shy, preoccupied, cautious and private.

Meaning
Financial prosperity, possessive, stingy, financial security.

In a reading
This card reflects the questioner's wish for financial security and for wanting to keep what they have.

Reversed
There may be financial loss, or alternatively, the questioner will need to invest money if they want to accumulate it.

Five of Pentacles

Principle
Loss.

Feelings
Survival, hard done by, self-destruct, self-pity.

Meaning
Unemployment, self-pity, lack of money, being out in the cold, can't take responsibility.

In a reading
This card indicates feelings of being victimised, and the subject feels as though they are out in the cold. This is a time to be responsible for decisions of the past, pick up the pieces and continue towards the light. All is not lost because valuable experience has been gained and the person is better equipped for the future.

Reversed
The questioner has started looking at the bigger picture, and they have put the past behind them. They are looking for a better way, and difficult times are over.

Six of Pentacles

Principle
Prosperity.

Feelings
Generous, giving, helping.

Meaning
Charity, giving away money, receiving charity, bribery.

In a reading
The subject has reached a point of material success and is now able to help others. Alternatively, they will receive a handout.

Reversed
The card can mean the person puts others' needs before their own, so they must identify their own needs and ensure they are met. By doing this, they show others how to look after themselves. If they choose to lend money, they mustn't expect it back.

Seven of Pentacles

Principle
Profit.

Feelings
Pensive, a risk-taker, always wanting more and never satisfied.

Meaning
Harvest, taking a gamble, working hard. The questioner shouldn't give up because there will be opportunities for success shortly.

In a reading
A lot of hard work has been done, but this is an excellent time to review their situation and decide if enough is enough, or if there is anything that could be done to ensure further growth.

Reversed
Financial insecurity or someone has focused too much on work and needs to keep some energy back for themselves and get a life.

Eight of Pentacles

Principle
Purpose.

Feelings
Diligent worker, thorough, likes to be alone, methodical.

Meaning
Self-employment, manual labour, new skills or courses, own creative energy.

In a reading
The person is creative and has acquired the skills necessary to create the life they want. They may be self-employed or planning to become self-employed, and if so, they will be successful.

Reversed
This is not a good time to become self-employed. Some special skills training might be necessary.

NINE OF PENTACLES

Principle
Culmination.

Feelings
Independence, self-assurance, taste, self-cantered, self-worth.

Meaning
Growth, prosperity, likes solitude, selfish with money.

In a reading
The subject is successful and wants to enjoy the finer things in life. Nothing is getting in their way of doing so.

Reversed
The questioner needs to re-evaluate personal possessions and goals.

TEN OF PENTACLES

Ten of Pentacles

Principle
Wealth.

Feelings
Protects what he has, wealthy, content.

Meaning
Large financial transactions, jealousy, family considerations, something inherited, perhaps a characteristic.

In a reading
The subject has achieved their goals and are happy. They have wisdom, and they have family and friends around them. If not, there is a positive change ahead. An inheritance or gift is likely. Money will be coming in.

Reversed
No time to take risks; the focus needs to be on repairing family relationships.

Chapter Ten:
The Court Cards

The Minor Arcana symbolises the various stages of life and the external influences that surround us. The Court cards represent aspects of ourselves and those around us, including family, friends, teachers, or colleagues. These people influence our values, beliefs, thought processes and decisions, both consciously and unconsciously. Each Court card represents a personality type. It can also show how we are currently dealing with a situation, or how we tell ourselves we ought to deal with a problem and describe those who may influence the situation.

Something slightly difficult to grasp is that all the Court cards characterise universal energy, and they can apply to either sex when associated with those around us. Each individual Court card is also tempered by the power of its suit, in addition to incorporating the energy of its associated astrological sign. This makes the Court cards multi-faceted, thus reflecting our human natures.

The card images in this book use the modern suit names: Swords, Cups, Wands and Pentacles. Other decks use different names like Chalices, Goblets, Rods and a few more as well. Choose a deck with names that suit you.

Traditional Tarot In Focus

PAGES

These cards represent the adolescent energy, new learning and the naïve novice, who can be full of self-doubt. They can also represent young and unmarried people who are usually aged fifteen to twenty-five.

PAGE OF SWORDS

Principle
Vigilance.

Feelings:
Irritating, petty, immature.

Meaning
Irritating, minor setbacks, nosiness, people one cannot trust, the inner critic and immaturity.

Astrology
Gemini. Two-faced, multi-faceted, inquisitive, superficial, social, restless and inconsistent.

Careers
Using inherent skills, communication, information industry, research, telesales, spying.

Physical description
White races, either very fair or very dark. Striking, good looking but with a severe expression. Slim and active.
Other races, attractive, slim, highly active, could have a serious expression or even a cross one.

Personality traits
Intelligent, has up-to-date news, sharp and smart, but not necessarily friendly. Could be training for a profession, for

journalism, broadcasting or the military. Quick moving and good at martial arts.

In a reading
Beware the inner critic and the little voice that continually undermines. When faced with adversity, learn to do things differently; otherwise, the pattern will be repeated until the lesson is learnt. Young people bearing gifts should not be trusted.

Reversed
Someone around is deliberately putting a spanner in the works. Identify who it is and cut them out. Confidence is improving.

Traditional Tarot In Focus

PAGE OF CUPS

Page of Cups

Principle
Messenger, a service rendered.

Feelings
Flamboyant, dreamy, vivid imagination, flirtatious.

Meaning
Messages of love and romance, vivid imagination, artistic, friendly.

Astrology
Pisces. Impressionable, imaginative, dreamer, self-effacing, confused.

Careers
Artist, writer, singer, psychic, youth worker or carer.

Physical description
White races, light brown hair, fair complexion, blue eyes, good looking. Other races, gentle appearance, friendly smile, somewhat round face and good looking.

Personality traits
Gentle, loving, artistic, insightful. Interested in poetry and the arts, dreamy at times, yet courageous when courage is needed.

In a reading
A person is in the individual's life or about to enter it, who will offer assistance that is safe to accept. This person is sensitive and intuitive.

Reversed
Beware because there is a false friend who will take advantage of your friendship.

10: The Court Cards

PAGE OF WANDS

Principle
Helpful information.

Feelings
Outspoken, extrovert, knows where he is going.

Meaning
Messages about new options opening, announcements, travel and looking ahead.

Astrology
Aries. Self-expression, urgency and initiative. Also, impulsive, selfish, fool-hardy, a survivor.

Career
Creative work, such as artist, musician, activist, charity worker, or work in the media.

Physical description
White races, light brown, fair or red hair, blue eyes.
Other races, round face, great smile, bright eyes.

Personality traits
A young person or a likeable stranger who is helpful, mild-mannered, friendly, polite, adaptable, industrious, enthusiastic and impulsive. They may be hyperactive with little staying power, and mat be easily bored.

In a reading
This is a trusted friend who is devoted to the questioner's interests. Their intentions will be honourable, so they can be trusted, even when talking on behalf of someone else. This card suggests that the questioner wants things to change, and it signals the individual

needs to break free of oppression or stagnation in business or find a solution to problems. Change is in the air, and a new approach is at hand. This could come through a friend who will help the subject see the light or attain a new perspective.

Reversed

This card's moral qualities turn into irritability, and while this person may look trustworthy, they will be dishonest. They can't keep a confidence, so they will lie and spread gossip. Alternatively, this card can talk of a delay or change of residence.

10: The Court Cards

PAGE OF PENTACLES

Principle
Good news.

Feelings
Optimism, clerical matters to deal with, must focus on detail and takes nothing at face value.

Meaning
New financial opportunity, a card of study, a plodder rather than a racer.

Astrology
Virgo. Service, discrimination, efficiency, conscientiousness, submissiveness, pedantry.

Career
Practical careers such as working with the hands and working out of doors. Can be an apprentice, gardener, dressmaker, cook, builder or electrician.

Physical description
White races, young person, dark-haired, introverted and probably a Virgo or other earth sign.
Other races, similar type as above with attractive features other than the teeth, which might be too prominent.

Personality traits
Action orientated and wanting to create a positive change. Committed to security. Hard-working, conscientious and responsible. This person is conventional, leaving nothing to chance, and is trustworthy and steadfast.

In a reading
Not the most practical of people because the Page still has a lot to learn. A new dimension is going to be added to the questioner's life. A new project may well be in the offing, or an event that will bring a new level of appreciation is on the way.

Reversed
This person is likely to waste opportunities.

10: The Court Cards

KNIGHTS

Knights represent those who are actively striving for goals, and they often need to prove themselves and show themselves they are good at what they do. Usually aged twenty-five to middle age.

KNIGHT OF SWORDS

Principle
Warning.

Feelings
Speedy, unreliable.

Meaning
Dashing in and out, impulsive, smooth, smart talker.

Astrology
Aquarius. Detachment, rebellion, reform, idealism, objective, scientific, erratic, gregarious, eccentric.

Career
Action orientated work, soldier, doctor, journalist, developer.

Physical description
White races, brown hair, grey, hazel or penetrating blue eyes. Other races, tall, slim, speaks slowly, penetrating eyes.

Personality Traits
Charismatic, powerful and intelligent. A good friend but a dangerous enemy. He is easily bored and keeps turning up like a bad penny.

In a reading
Often represents an ex-partner who keeps breezing in and breezing

out of the subject's life, usually creating havoc. They see themselves as the gallant hero who is strong, brave and capable of succeeding at everything they do. However, they want everything yesterday, which makes them unreliable.

Reversed
This person is reckless, sneaky, sly and deceitful. Has little staying power but is fierce in action. This knight rarely finishes what they start.

KNIGHT OF CUPS

Principle
Kindness, an offer of love.

Feelings
Dainty, romantic, optimistic, gentle, carefree, pedantic.

Meaning
A lover coming in or going out, new horizons, a social card.

Astrology
Pisces. Compassionate, receptive, malleable, imaginative, dreamer, transcendent.

Career
People orientated roles, human resources, care worker, nurse, artist, musician, poet, not for profit organizations.

Physical description
White races, light brown to fair hair, fair complexion and casual appearance.
Other races, slim, graceful, casual rather than formal in approach.

Personality traits
Enthusiastic, passionate, amiable, well-travelled, often poetic and graceful.

In a reading
Often indicates a romantic relationship or some other favourable offer coming into the subject's life which they should accept because it will be good. The questioner or someone around them is a caring individual with a sense of adventure. They are sensitive

and trust their feelings. The heart rules the head. The individual should trust their feelings in any situation. There should be a change for the better soon because things are looking up.

Reversed

A moody, jealous person or a situation in which the questioner should look at logically rather than emotionally.

10: The Court Cards

KNIGHT OF WANDS

Principle
Adventure.

Feelings
Loves a challenge, adventurous, forward-looking, optimistic and exciting.

Meaning
Travel, moving, relocation, gaps in wisdom, impetuous, attractive.

Astrology
Leo. Loyal, proud, enthusiastic, generous, opinionated, playful and dramatic.

Career
Active and competitive jobs, often involving travel. Paramedic, pilot, salesperson, filmmaker or a young entrepreneur.

Physical description
White races, light brown, blond or red hair, blue eyes, a robust, intense look, often with a ruddy complexion from many outdoor activities.
Other races, medium height, well built, friendly smile, small eyes, soft hair.

Personality Traits
Always eager to help. May take calculated risks but is trustworthy and honourable. First impressions count with them because they can be quick to love or hate.

In a reading
Represents mental intuition, an impetuous nature, and a generous

friend or lover. They actively pursue their vision with an abandon that is characteristic of the impulsive astrological sign of Leo. This person loves action, and they are well-liked and ambitious. Their temperament is engaging, and although they move quickly, their actions always make sense, if only in hindsight.

Reversed
This person likes discord, arguments, strife and trouble just for the sake of it. They are destructive. Can also mean delays to any plans, mostly involving travel or business.

Knight of Pentacles

Principle
Having potential.

Feelings
Steadfast, dependable, serious and genuine.

Meaning
Messages of financial opportunities. A slow, practical approach, analytical, clever with hands.

Astrology
Taurus. Steadfast, materialistic, practical, thorough, stubborn, patient and self-indulgent.

Career
Practical routine work, accounts, admin, legal work involving property matters or banking.

Physical description
White races, a dark-haired, dark-eyed person who is well built and strong.
Other races, a stocky, well-built person with very dark eyes.

Personality traits
A person with the patience to accomplish tasks. Reliable due to their sense of responsibility. Very traditional, smart with money, patient and hardworking. They are very much about fulfilling obligations.

In a reading
The subject seems to be pondering their next move. Perhaps the goal seems to get further away rather than nearer. The subject needs

to look back at what has already been achieved and keep going one step at a time. If not the person themselves, someone will be coming into their life to assist with the next step.

Reversed

Beware of anyone helping, because their motives are not honourable.

10: The Court Cards

QUEENS

Queens represent authority and achievement. They have accepted themselves and no longer strive because they allow things to happen in their own time. They are intuitive and wise. Queens represent people between the ages of forty and sixty.

QUEEN OF SWORDS

Principle
Intellectual manipulation or mental chaos.

Feelings
Lonely, astute, detached, courage, integrity and tenacity. Respected and admired.

Meaning
Likes to be alone, single, divorced or widowed, focused, controlled.

Astrology
Libra. Diplomatic, perfectionist, over-analytical, judgmental and determined.

Career
Lecturer, professor, manager.

Physical description
White races, red or dark brown hair, grey, hazel or blue eyes. Graceful.
Other races, slim, good looking but with a serious expression, possibly light eyes.

Personality traits
An influential, intelligent person. Very independent and rational, if not analytical. Keeps her head in a crisis and is an excellent

advocate on behalf of others. They should never be underestimated. Likely to be in a position of authority and is more than capable of making decisions. Probably separated, divorced or widowed.

In a reading
Intellectual ability to judge and discern impartially without the influence of emotions. Someone stern and unforgiving. They hate being told what to do and need to know everything before deciding to do whatever is right in their own eyes. A very strong-willed and ambitious person who is particularly good at solving problems. They can be very altruistic and diplomatic. A good communicator and excellent teacher, but can be over-analytical and critical.

Reversed
This suggests the questioner may think more with their heart than their head. They may be more emotionally involved than they need to be with a situation or issue, and it may distort their perception of the situation. Time to use the head a little more and look purposely at the situation before making any decisions. It can also mean they should beware of a cold, intelligent person who will make a dangerous enemy.

10: The Court Cards

QUEEN OF CUPS

Principle
Emotional security.

Feelings
Emotional, dramatic, creative, visionary and perceptive.

Meaning
Secure, loving woman, compassionate, artistic, sensitive, and aloof.

Astrology
Cancer. Emotional, nurturing, vulnerable, defensive, tenacious, sensitive, intuitive.

Career
Roles involving sensitivity such as healer, nurse, psychic or counsellor.

Physical description
In white races, light brown or blond hair, fair complexion, a beautiful woman, with expressive eyes.
Other races, a beautiful woman with a rounded body and lovely eyes.

Personality traits
Warm, loving, sociable, good-natured, devoted, sympathetic, honest, loyal and artistic.

In a reading
Imaginative and artistically gifted person who is romantic with an affectionate outlook, and creates a cosmopolitan atmosphere around them. They lack common sense, but are highly intuitive

and psychic. They have a nurturing personality, so they genuinely care about the well-being of other people. They can also be unfathomable because still waters run deep, but they have a sympathetic ear and are an excellent shoulder to cry on. They keep their emotions under control while having oceans of compassion and empathy for others. They dislike thoughtlessness and inappropriate behaviour.

Reversed
A person who changes their feelings and opinions without reason or cause. They can be perverse and given to hysteria. They can lead others to destruction in pursuit of their idle fantasies. They cannot be relied on or depended on at all.

10: The Court Cards

QUEEN OF WANDS

Principle
Inspiration.

Feelings
Likes animals and being outdoors. An outgoing, kind, good all-rounder, who is strong, happy, optimistic, secure and friendly.

QUEEN OF WANDS

Meaning
A kind, generous person, often self-employed, trustworthy, lucky.

Astrology
Leo. Loyal, generous, playful, benevolent, dignified, self-assured and caring.

Career
Teacher, leader, self-employed worker.

Physical Description
White races, light brown, blond or red-haired, blue-eyed person. Other races, medium height and weight, happy smile, bright eyes, great hair.

Personality traits
Intelligent, dignified, prosperous loving, happy person who is full of self-confidence. They offer help and inspiration that you can trust. They are lively, active, warm-natured, a good organizer and very practical. They run a business or hold a responsible position. They are also a lover of nature. Very grounded for a fire sign.

In a reading
This person loves the country and prefers to live there. They are

fair and capable in their dealings with others. They are creative in body and mind and make both a promising businessperson and a good homemaker. They enjoy their social life and are often seen as charming. They are very protective of others.

Reversed

This person is dominating or bitter, and embodies the overbearing matriarchal type. They can be cruel, with a dry sense of humour. This person may be paranoid, believing everyone is out to get them.

10: The Court Cards

QUEEN OF PENTACLES

Principle
Security.

Feelings
Safe, secure, appreciative, nurturing, good sixth sense.

Meaning
Financial security, independence, generosity, materialistic, liking luxuries.

Astrology
Taurus. Well off, steadfast, practical, secure, possessive, patient, and hedonistic.

Career
Business owner, senior manager, solicitor, barrister, financier.

Physical description
All racial types. Dark haired person with a cheerful and robust constitution.

Personality traits
This character is practical and energetic. They are the original Earth Parent. They are secure; they enjoy luxury and appreciate abundance. They are generous, sincere, with a good head for business and are generally very caring.

In a reading
The questioner needs to learn from a caring, wise person who is already in their life or about to enter their life. A lot of good things will come out of this.

Reversed
Beware of people bearing gifts because they come with a hefty price tag. The subject already has what they need, and they can work out the answers for themselves.

10: The Court Cards

KINGS

Kings represent authority and achievement. They are decisive and they rule wisely, although they often see themselves as being right. They can be fixed in their ways depending upon the element of their suit.

KING OF SWORDS

Principle
Mental strength and power.

Feelings
Impulsive, changeable, impatient, rushing, unreliable.

Meaning
Likes to be alone. A bachelor, divorcee or widower who is highly intelligent.

Astrology
Gemini. Multifaceted, adaptable, inquisitive, versatile, capricious, cunning and restless.

Career
Lawyer, professor, technology, scientist, astronomer.

Physical Description
White races, dark brown hair, grey, hazel or blue eyes.
Other races, slim with a severe expression on a relatively narrow face.

Personality Traits
Their application of intelligence has made their heart cold. They understand human nature and use the knowledge for their own advantage. They are in a position of trust and authority. They are

logical and calm; they dislike overt displays of emotion and requires mental stimulation. they can be like a parent, spouse, employer, teacher, lawyer, doctor or professional advisor.

In a reading
This character is the epitome of intellectual power, representing judgment, command and leadership. Their character suggests the stern kind of leadership seen in a judge, lawyer or a military commander whose emotions must be kept in check under the pressure of battle. They are often over-analytical.

Reversed
This card can suggest the misuse of authority and drive. It represents manipulation to fulfil selfish needs. This may be an intelligent older person who likes to show off their intelligence while being very patronizing and critical of others. They are always right without respecting the views of others. They are calculating, obstinate and capable of using ultimate evil to achieve their aims and desires.

10: The Court Cards

KING OF CUPS

Principle
Honourable, sensitive.

Feelings
Sensitive demonstrative, gentle and emotionally secure.

Meaning
Keeps emotions close to the chest, aloof and inadvertently patronising.

Astrology
Scorpio. Mastery, intensity, power, magnetism, transformative, mysterious, vindictive, controlling or suspicious.

Career
Consultant, business owner, vicar or priest, lawyer, CEO of a charity, counsellor.

Physical description
White races, light brown hair, fair complexion, clear liquid eyes. Other races, medium build, lovely complexion, expressive and fascinating eyes.

Personality traits
They are hard to understand, but they are trustworthy. They have achieved something in life. They are friendly, loving, sensuous, and intelligent, combined with strong intuition. The person is creative and enjoys the arts and comforts of life. Responsible and generous, an older businessperson in a responsible position. A kindly parental figure.

In a reading

They are masters of their own feelings and they control their emotions, yet They are compassionate and kind. Strong bonds in a relationship based on temperance and understanding. They are considerate and willing to take responsibility. They may be interested in the arts and sciences, and they enjoy quiet power. Commands respect but not always love. They have achieved their position in life by using their brains rather than their brawn. They avoid taking people into their confidence, and they rarely express their emotions. They prefer to work behind the scenes.

Reversed

This card suggests that someone around the questioner is not to be trusted. Perhaps the subject needs to realise that they are not being as honest as they should be in the situation.

10: The Court Cards

KING OF WANDS

Principle
Honour.

Feelings
Trustworthy, reliable, capable, sceptical, wise.

Meaning
Materialistic, trusting, good all-rounder holds a position of authority, wise.

Astrology
Sagittarius. Adventurous, idealistic, freedom, spontaneous, tactless, extravagant, restless.

Career
Leader, politician, management, consultant.

Physical description
White races, light brown, fair or red hair, a blue-eyed older person who is athletic, strong and healthy.
Other races, an older person who is tall, fit, strong and capable.

Personality traits
Creative, self-expressive, passionate, showy, theatrical, and they like to gamble. They have power and influence and know when to act and when to wait. They have a good sense of humour and create harmonious relationships with most of those who encounter them. They are honourable in an old-fashioned sense. They have probably travelled widely and have gained much wisdom, so they make excellent advisors.

In a reading
Represents the epitome of the qualities associated with the element

of fire. These include strength, leadership, creativity, vision and the motivation to bring that creative vision into reality. They are the type of person people naturally flock to and follow. They get things done, often by getting others to do it for them! For the most part, they are charming, responsible, loyal, entertaining, witty, honest, conscientious and generous. They love their home, and they love family life. If they are pushed or provoked, they will act without hesitation, even though it may be hard for them, because they can see both sides of any situation.

Reversed
This person has a ruthless streak, and they don't care in the least about others' feelings. In love, they represent a delightful flirtation that could wreak emotional havoc. They are only suitable for limited liaisons, holiday romances or delicious brief encounters. They are completely unable to see the point of view of others. They have no tolerance, they are intolerant and narrow-minded with deep-set prejudices.

10: The Court Cards

KING OF PENTACLES

Principle
Wealth.

Feelings
Superficial, materialistic, possessive or a superior attitude.

Meaning
Someone who hoards, miserly, wealthy, remains isolated.

Astrology
Capricorn. Authoritarian, cautious, disciplined, conservative, dutiful, pessimistic, prudent, patient, narrow-minded, conventional or callous.

Careers
Business owners and middle management within business and finance, leaders of industry.

Physical description
All racial types, a dark-haired person usually middle-aged or elderly.

Personality traits
They are devoted friends who are trustworthy and loyal. They care deeply for their family and are slow to anger, but they are not very demonstrative. They have a controlled form of energy and purpose.

In a reading
The subject is rich, or they will achieve great wealth. Alternatively, there is someone around the individual who has great wealth and is willing to assist them.

Reversed
The questioners need to trust themselves and take back their power. Security lies in the confidence to cope with what life throws at them rather than trying to obtain material wealth.

Chapter Eleven: Giving a Reading

If possible, set aside a place in your home, because by using the same spot over and over, you build up the energy that will reinforce and strengthen your practice. If you meditate or pray, you could carry out these activities here as they harmonise with the Tarot in spirit and intent. You may wish to have items nearby that have a special meaning for you, such as shells, stones, crystals and plants. A talisman or a religious icon may help you shift your focus away from the mundane to the inspirational. Consider pictures and other items that appeal to your senses, such as flowers, incense, candles, textured materials and quiet, meditative music. Although these touches are excellent, the only thing you really need is somewhere to lay out the cards, and you can use either a table or the floor. There is a grounded feeling about giving readings on the floor, but if this is uncomfortable for you, it would be better to sit at a table and keep your feet on the ground.

Frankly, all you really need is to take the cards out of the box and use them. That's the important part!

PREPARING YOUR CARDS

There are no hard or fast rules when preparing a new deck, and neither is there a right or a wrong way to do it. An easy way to energise a new deck is just to turn the cards face up and count them, whilst setting your intention that the cards answer questions for the highest good.

There are many ways of getting ready to give a reading, and they are all fine. Many people ask their clients to shuffle the deck whilst holding their question in their mind, then cut the deck putting the lower part of the cut on the top, and then dealing the required number of cards.

Some don't cut the deck at all, while others ask the client to cut them into three piles and then choose which stack to use. Some prefer to shuffle and fan the cards in front of the client and ask him to randomly pick the required number of cards, using his left hand. (The left hand is guided by the right, intuitive, part of the brain). Some readers decide they don't want anyone else to touch their cards, so they shuffle and pick cards for the client. Most do give the deck to the client and ask them to shuffle, cut and pick the cards though, but however you choose to prepare your cards for a reading is entirely up to you.

FORMING QUESTIONS

So far, I have shown you how to work with individual cards and gradually learn their meanings, and I have shown how the energies in a card influence us. Now I will introduce the idea of asking questions and combining the cards into what are known as spreads.

Let us assume you've been drawing one card each day and asking what it will mean to you for that day, but now is the time to take this further by asking specific questions. Take care with the answers to questions such as, "Is it *good* for me?" "Are they *nice*?" "Is this the *right* person for me?" because someone you meet now may be the "right" person for you at this time or for a specific purpose, but they may not work out well in the long run. Think of issues you may have within your life or with different people and see what the cards have to say about them.

EITHER/OR QUESTIONS

Consider a particular area of your life while shuffling the deck and drawing two cards, one for the near future and the second for the longer term. You may have a question such as: "I am fed up with my job, so would it be better for me to stay where I am for now or look for a better job?" Look at the two cards and see what you should do regarding your career situation soon and in the more distant future.

Similarly, "There are two houses I like, but which is the best choice for me right at this moment in time and is it right for my own highest good and the highest good of all concerned. Would

11: Giving a Reading

this be Rose Cottage or Lily Cottage?" With your question in mind, draw one for the likely short-term result and one for the likely longer-term outcome for each option. Notice how you feel about the answers. This will be important in the future as well because when you are working with clients, we know they have questions they want to be answered, but you will be at a disadvantage, because you don't know what questions they have in their minds, yet you will still be expected to answer them!

Sometimes the things that are on the client's mind become apparent from the cards themselves, but we often need to ask ourselves (and the cards) inner questions. Practising by asking and answering questions is an essential part of learning to read the Tarot. In my experience, the more focussed and specific the question, the more obvious the answer. It determines not only the answer you receive but the way you go about approaching the interpretation. The question provides a structure for your intuition to work on, so it's important to ask clear and precise questions, using words that mean something to you.

Information from the cards needs to be interpreted according to the question being asked, so don't make the questions vague. An example of a vague question would be: "Will I be moving to a new house?" This kind of question needs precision, so make it: "will I be moving to a new house in the next three months?"

Learning to formulate clear inner questions is an essential part of all Tarot readings. When working with clients, you will soon notice that most people are interested in specific areas of their lives, such as their job, relationships, family, money, health, moving home and so on. Having plenty of practice at this stage will enable you to develop a list of inner questions that you keep in mind.

READING FOR YOURSELF

Many people feel reading for yourself can be misleading as you are too close to a situation and it is difficult to be objective. It is a fact that we all tend to see what we want to see rather than what really is there. However, often the only way to practise and get to

Traditional Tarot In Focus

know how to interpret the cards in different situations *is* to read for yourself. If you guard against seeing what you want to see, it is often helpful in opening your awareness to other options. You will need to remember to keep all the possible meanings in mind and trust your intuition rather than what you would like the reading to mean. Reading for yourself can help you see things differently. It opens avenues and choices by showing you what is happening in your situation and where your current behaviour will take you, while also showing you any unconscious undercurrents, allowing you to consider ways of creating different outcomes. This is precisely what clients will expect of you when you read for them.

Chapter Twelve:
Spreads

There are so many different spreads that we can only look at one or two of them here. Bear in mind that you can create your own spreads, because all you need to do is designate what the position you place each card in will mean.

When practising these spreads, I recommend that you keep notes of the questions you ask and your interpretation of the cards. Review your notes at the end of the day, week or month to judge your accuracy, and see what you could have learned with hindsight. It is often at the review stage that you discover better ways of interpreting the cards.

SIMPLE THREE-CARD SPREADS

Designate what each position will represent; for instance, we can assign the positions to past, present and future. This useful spread is short and to the point. So now, think of an issue or a question, choose three cards at random and lay the cards from left to right in the following order:

Past
Present
Future

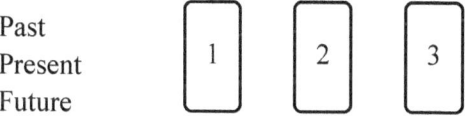

Each card depicts the energy within the situation in relation to its position, but you should start to spot the combination of the energies of all three cards and how they affect each other, along with your feelings about them. Ask yourself if there is a predominant colour or theme in all the cards, or anything else that shows how they relate to each other.

Traditional Tarot In Focus

You could also use the three-card spread to represent three different areas of your life, as follows:

Love
Money
Health

| 1 | 2 | 3 |

The three positions can also be used to represent a specific issue:
Consider a setback or blockage
The likely outcome
The action that needs to be taken

| 1 | 2 | 3 |

Another version might be to use four cards and lay them the same way looking at the following:
Your physical state for the day
Your emotional state for the day
Your mental state for the day
Your spiritual objective for the day

| 1 | 2 | 3 | 4 |

As you can see, each position can mean anything you want it to. In one way, this can be applied to any spread, but many spreads have well-established meanings for each position, and we will look at one or two of these later.

12: Spreads

WEEKLY SPREAD

You can create a weekly spread by drawing seven cards and asking what the week ahead will be like, either by looking at the week as a whole or designating each card to represent what you need to focus on during each day of the week. This is an excellent way to learn how the cards interact with each other and start the process of telling their story.

TELLING A STORY

Before we progress to the more complex spreads that you will use for yourself, family, friends, and eventually your clients, you need to begin practising telling a story. As we know, the Major Arcana takes us through the rites of passage that we pass through while we learn and grow during our earthly existence, but we need to apply this knowledge to our readings. By putting it in story-form and following the cards through the questioner's past and present, along with the conscious and unconscious influences and options for the future, it becomes easy for the subject to understand. Start with a short description of the client's personality, because this shows you are connecting to their energy, then talk a little about the past, and then look at the issues that are facing the client in the present and suggest probable outcomes.

Remember that everything you experience whilst doing a reading is relevant in some way, even when a client does not readily accept it. The only way forward is to practise, and with each reading you give, you will discover more about how you receive messages. You will see what they mean to you and to others, and over time you will perfect your own individual strength and style. Telling the story is crucial because it needs to make sense to the client.

DRAWING A PICTURE WITH LANGUAGE AND METAPHOR

Language means different things to different people, especially if you are dealing with people from other cultures. Metaphors often make it easier for people to understand what they are being told, but some metaphors don't translate to people of different cultures, so keep it simple. Some archetypal concepts make sense to everyone, for instance, a *ladder*. For example, when describing the Queen of Wands, you might say they are a person who has achieved a lot, and that they are working towards becoming the Queen of all they survey. Wands tend to talk about work and career matters, so you can ask the cards to tell you whether this particular person is happy in their career and whether they are climbing the ladder of success. You could ask whether they will still be satisfied when they have reached the top of the ladder. Remember that this energy could equally apply to any gender.

Another archetype that is easy to grasp is that of a butterfly. For example, the Fool card depicts a naive young person who is about to embark on life, but when this card turns up in the middle of an adult's reading, the card points to the start of a new cycle. Many people get confused and worried about this idea. Still, by relating the card to a butterfly's lifecycle, you can describe how a butterfly grows out of the caterpillar's cocoon and discards what is no longer wanted. Alternatively, this could symbolise spinning a cocoon of protection against the hard knocks in life.

RELATIONSHIP SPREADS

Relationships are a big part of our lives, and they are often the focus of clients' enquiries. You will find two different relationship spreads below. Remember we are in a relationship with everyone we deal with, so it doesn't have to be a romantic relationship, but a connection to a friend, colleague, sibling, parent, child, neighbour, and even the relationship between our conscious and unconscious selves.

Spread One
Start by reading down the first column to see what has influenced the client in the past, what is happening now and the likely outcome in the future, or perhaps some action that the client needs to take.

12: Spreads

Do the same with the second column to see how the other person in their life is behaving and why this is the case.

Check the third column to see how the situation is likely to turn out for the client and for the other person in their life.

Read across each column for a more in-depth view of what has happened to both people, what is happening now, and the best way forward for all concerned.

By adding more rows, you could also check out the conscious and unconscious desires, thus giving an even deeper reading.

THE CLIENT	OTHER PERSON	ACTION NEEDED/ OUTCOME
PAST	PAST	CAUSE
PRESENT	PRESENT	PRESENT
FUTURE	FUTURE	FUTURE

Spread Two

THE CELTIC CROSS SPREAD

As with the history of Tarot, no one is exactly sure where this spread originated. It first appeared in a book published in 1910 called the *Pictorial Key to the Tarot* by Arthur Edward Waite, who, with artist Pamela Colman Smith created the most popular deck on the market today, which is known as the Rider Waite deck. This deck and this spread are the most widely used by Tarot readers across the world; it gives a very in-depth reading.

Whether you shuffle the cards for the questioner or whether your client does it themselves, the shuffler must think about the questions they want to be answered. Some people cut the cards and place the bottom pile and on the top while others just leave them. Those who don't want anyone else to shuffle their cards, fan them out and ask the subject to pick ten cards at random with their left hand and the cards are then laid out as per the diagram below and read in order.

Some people also use what is known as a *"significator"* card. This is placed face up in the middle, and it represents the client.

The first card is placed on top of it, and it is said to show what is *"covering"* the questioner. In plain English, this means, the circumstances in which they find themselves or the problem that needs to be solved. This is not an easy spread to get to grips with, but it is well worth the time and effort.

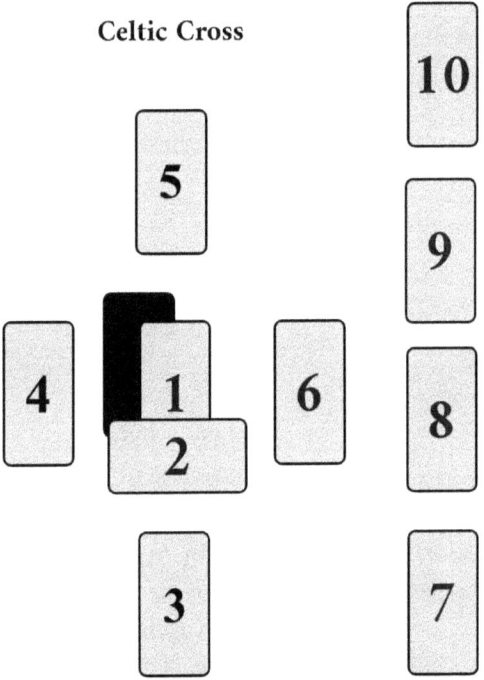

Celtic Cross

The dark square stands for the significator, which is a card that represents the client. You don't have to use a significator; indeed, few professional Tarot readers bother with this as it is time-consuming. If you decide to use one, you can choose a Court card that links with the client's zodiac sign, or one that you think is representative of the client.

12: Spreads

1. The situation the client finds themselves in or the one they need to investigate.
2. More about the things that are bothering the client currently.
3. The best that the client can expect as an outcome to his current situation.
4. The distant past.
5. The recent past, as it impinges on the current situation.
6. The near future.
7. How the client affects the people and circumstances that are around them.
8. How the people or circumstances around the client affect them.
9. The client's hopes and wishes, or fears and worries relating to the situation.
10. The eventual outcome.

THE HOROSCOPE SPREAD

This is a big spread, but it is easier to cope with than the Celtic Cross. It is based on what astrologers call the natal chart, but you don't need to be an astrologer to use it. Each of the twelve positions links to the twelve astrological houses. However, this can also be used as a timing device; each position can also be used to signify a month, giving a reading for the coming year. The twelve cards are laid out as a circle. An astrologer would start at the nine o'clock position and work around the system in an anti-clockwise direction, mimicking the way an astrology chart is read. Some readers start in the nine o'clock position and call this Aries or April and work through the coming year or two that way.

The Astrological Houses
1. Personality, ego, control issues.
2. Practical issues home, money, life values.
3. Communication and short journeys.
4. Security issues, mother and private world.
5. Inner child, hobbies, fun.

6 Learning, health, charity work, outside influences.
7 Relationships, partnerships.
8 Karma, transformation, mysterious endings and beginnings.
9 Distant journeys, travel, wisdom, higher education.
11 Work, Destiny, ambition, how others see the client.
12 Hopes and wishes, what makes the client happy, social life, friendships, vision.
13 Latent talents, hidden potential, mystical psychic matters, what stops the client from moving forward.

Creating your Own Spreads

The spreads in this book were all created by individuals who shared them with others, and over time many readers found they work very well. However, they are not the only way to work. Anyone can create their own spread for any purpose. Whether you are modifying one that you have come across elsewhere or creating something completely new, it all works.

Many new spreads have come into being, for use with the myriad of new oracle cards that are now on the market.

Using the Major Arcana alone makes it easy to see the big picture rather than getting bogged down in unnecessary detail and being unable to see the wood for the trees.

12: Spreads

SPECIALLY CREATED SPREADS

Remember to ask the Tarot "what, how and why" questions, decide what in general you want to know, and then design a spread to answer them. For instance, in my nine-card spread, I lay it out like a diamond, with the top card being the main issue followed by other influences, in addition to the underlying pressures. Each position also indicates a month, with number one showing what will happen in one month's time, and number nine being nine months.

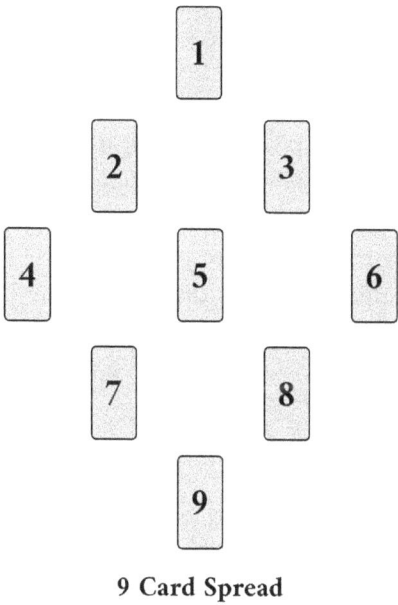

9 Card Spread

The top five cards become what I call the *Soul Qualities Spread*, showing the kind of soul or spirit that the client has. The remaining cards become *The Life Purpose Spread*, because this gives the client an overview of his life's purpose. You might also want to drill down by asking "what if" questions, and perhaps drawing an extra card or two to discover more information regarding possible outcomes or to clarify a point.

A Complex Spread

I use a spread devised by my Tarot teacher, Jackie Barnes. It is a very in-depth spread and can be used for everything. It is based on the Celtic Cross, but it uses pairs of cards rather than single cards, and each position has more than one role. I use one Major Arcana card and one Minor Arcana card in each position. Finally, take the remaining Major Arcana cards and place them in a circle as if they were the numbers on a clock, then consider the major influence for each of the coming twelve months. By combining the two parts of this reading, you end up with an in-depth analysis.

The Undercurrent Card

Sometimes spreads are not always as straightforward as we would like them to be, so it can be useful to look at the undercurrent that has a bearing on the client's situation. The undercurrent card is the card that sits on the bottom of the pack after shuffling. Many readers take a quick glance at this card to get a feel for what a reading is about.

Conclusion

Now that you have this book on hand to help you understand the cards' meanings and how to use them, it is time to practise, practise, and practise. Only with lots of practice can you become a great reader. Even if you intend to use the cards purely for your own self-development or entertainment, the more you use them, the better you will become.

You may at some-point consider becoming professional. There are many laws appertaining to being a professional reader, depending upon the part of the world you live in and where you intend to practise. With the internet, you can have clients worldwide, using tools like Skype, Zoom, Facetime and WhatsApp. I highly recommend joining a professional organisation and finding out what laws govern the industry in your country. In England, there is MBS Professionals Ltd, with ethical guidelines and codes of conduct for professional consultants to follow, or the Spiritual Workers Association, which also offers codes of conduct and advice.

(MBS stands for Mind, Body and Spirit.)

There are also several other things you will need to investigate and consider before becoming professional, such as recording, emailing recordings to clients, insurance, disclaimers, and what you can and can't talk about. MBS Professionals Ltd can offer advice and the right kind of insurance at a reasonable price. Contact them at mbsprofessionals@gmail.com. However, you can also ask someone who already works in the field, as they will know the rules and regulations that apply in the country in which you live and wish to work. You may already know someone who gives readings, and they will be in an excellent position to advise you, but above all, enjoy your onward journey with the Tarot!

Joylina
joylina@joylina.com

Index

A
Adam and Eve 46
Alphonse XI 6
Astrological Houses 165
auras 11

B
Barnes, Jackie 168
Binah 38

C
Caduceus 29
Chakras 19
Charles VI 6, 7
Christian Virtues 6
Crone 34
Crowley, Aleister 7, 14
Crystal Tarot 14

D
Diamond Tarot 14

E
Egyptian Tarot 14
Either/Or Questions 156

F
Forming Questions 156
Fountain Tarot 14

G
Gebelin, Antoine Court de 7
General Medical Council 29
Gringonneur 7
Gringonneur, Jacquemin 6
gut feelings 12

H
Hermetic Tarot 14

I
insurance 169
Intuition 10

J
Jehovah 38
Johannes of Brefeld 6
Johannes Von Rheinfelden 6
Journey to Enlightenment 10

K
karmic number 28
King of Clubs 7
King of Hearts 7
King of Leon and Castile 6
Kundalini 30

L
Levi, Eliphas 7

M
Martiano da Tortona 6
Martinists 7
Master Numbers 24
Mathers, Samuel Liddell 7
MBS Professionals Ltd 169

Index

meditation, breathing 12
medium 11
Melchisedec 29
Menestrier 7
Murner, Thomas 7

O
Oceanic Tarot 14
Old Testament 54
Osho Zen Tarot 14

P
Pictorial Key to the Tarot 163
Pope 44
Preparing your Cards 155
psychic 11

Q
Qabala 7

R
Reading for Yourself 157
readings, daily 17
Rider Waite deck 163
Rider-Waite Tarot 8
rites of passage 9
Rituals 15
Rosicrucians 7

S
Sixth Sense 10
Smith, Pamela Colman 8
Spiritual Workers Association, 169
Spread, Celtic Cross 163
Spread, Complex 168
Spread, Horoscope 165
Spread, Weekly 161
Spreads, Relationship 162
Spreads, Specially Created 167
spreads, Three-Card 159
St Bernadino of Siena 6
Syrian Star Seed Tarot 14

T
Tarocchi 6
Ten Commandments 54
Thoth deck 14
Tora 54
Torah 38
Tree of Knowledge 46
Trumps 6

W
Waite, Arthur Edward 7, 8, 163

Y
YHVH 54

Z
Zero 24

www.ingramcontent.com/pod-product-compliance
Lightning Source LLC
Chambersburg PA
CBHW070541090426
42735CB00013B/3045